D1134335

meat
100 everyday recipes

First published in 2012
LOVE FOOD is an imprint of Parragon Books Ltd

Parragon
Queen Street House
4 Queen Street
Bath BA1 1HE, UK

www.parragon.com

ISBN: 978-1-4454-6635-4

Printed in China

Produced by Ivy Contract
Cover photography by Mike Cooper
Cover image home economy and food styling by Lincoln Jefferson

Notes for the Reader

This book uses both metric and imperial measurements. Follow the same units of measurement throughout; do not mix metric and imperial. All spoon measurements are level: teaspoons are assumed to be 5 ml, and tablespoons are assumed to be 15 ml. Unless otherwise stated, milk is assumed to be full fat, eggs and individual vegetables are medium, and pepper is freshly ground black pepper.

The times given are an approximate guide only. Preparation times differ according to the techniques used by different people and the cooking times may also vary from those given. Optional ingredients, variations or serving suggestions have not been included in the calculations.

Recipes using raw or very lightly cooked eggs should be avoided by infants, the elderly, pregnant women, convalescents and anyone suffering from an illness. Pregnant and breastfeeding women are advised to avoid eating peanuts and peanut products. Sufferers from nut allergies should be aware that some of the ready-made ingredients used in the recipes in this book may contain nuts. Always check the packaging before use.

meat

introduction

For many people, a meal simply isn't complete without the addition of meat. A rich source of nutritionally essential protein, meat can be healthy and highly satisfying. Meat has a texture and a rich savouriness that no other food can replicate, and for many people the inimitable taste of bacon or the sensation of taking a bite of melt-in-the-mouth steak is a culinary pleasure that is unsurpassed. Whether meat is a daily presence on your table, or you prefer to treat it as a special indulgence, this book can provide you with recipes to make both the cheaper and the more luxurious cuts of meat absolutely delicious. For example, hearty and wholesome pork and pasta bake is an excellent recipe to feed all the family without breaking the bank, whilst recipes for classic beef Wellington or roast goose with cinnamon-spiced red cabbage are perfect if you're planning a sumptuous feast.

Meat dishes can be made healthier by choosing leaner cuts, while using a griddle pan or grill rather than a flat pan can also help to reduce the saturated fat content of the dish. Choosing good-quality meat will not only improve the flavour and texture of your dinner, it is also more nutritionally valuable, so all round it's better to buy smaller portions of high-quality produce than fill up with poor-quality meat.

Preparing meat can be aided by having a very sharp knife, and it's a sensible idea to have a chopping board reserved specifically for it, which is never used for any other foodstuffs. Meat should always be kept in the refrigerator, and it's important to keep raw meat away from other cooked foods.

This book is divided into chapters for different types of meat, and within them you will find recipes for all tastes, and suitable for all occasions, from light lunch dishes such as chicken Caesar salad, to impressive meals for special occasions, like roast venison with brandy sauce – and everything in-between. This book will inspire you to try something a bit different, and provide you with the confidence to create a meat dish that is something really special.

beef & lamb

beef & bean soup

ingredients

serves 4

2 tbsp vegetable oil

1 large onion, finely chopped

2 garlic cloves, finely chopped

1 green pepper, deseeded
    and sliced

2 carrots, sliced

400 g/14 oz canned black-eyed
    beans

225 g/8 oz fresh beef mince

1 tsp each ground cumin, chilli
    powder and paprika

¼ cabbage, sliced

225 g/8 oz tomatoes, peeled
    and chopped

600 ml/1 pint beef stock

salt and pepper

method

1 Heat the oil in a large saucepan over a medium heat.
   Add the onion and garlic and cook, stirring frequently,
   for 5 minutes, or until softened. Add the pepper and
   carrots and cook for a further 5 minutes.

2 Meanwhile, drain the beans, reserving the liquid from
   the can. Place two thirds of the beans, reserving the
   remainder, in a food processor or blender with the
   bean liquid and process until smooth.

3 Add the beef to the saucepan and cook, stirring
   constantly, to break up any lumps, until well browned.
   Add the spices and cook, stirring, for 2 minutes. Add
   the cabbage, tomatoes, stock and puréed beans
   and season to taste with salt and pepper. Bring to
   the boil, then reduce the heat, cover and simmer for
   15 minutes, or until the vegetables are tender.

4 Stir in the reserved beans, cover and simmer for a
   further 5 minutes. Ladle the soup into warmed soup
   bowls and serve.

spicy beef & noodle soup

ingredients

serves 4

1 litre/1¾ pints beef stock
150 ml/5 fl oz vegetable or
    groundnut oil
85 g/3 oz rice vermicelli noodles
2 shallots, thinly sliced
2 garlic cloves, crushed
2.5-cm/1-inch piece fresh
    ginger, thinly sliced
225 g/8 oz piece fillet steak,
    cut into thin strips
2 tbsp green curry paste
2 tbsp Thai soy sauce
1 tbsp fish sauce
fresh coriander sprigs,
    to garnish

method

1 Pour the stock into a large saucepan and bring to the boil. Meanwhile, heat the oil in a wok or large frying pan. Add a third of the noodles and fry for 10–20 seconds, until they have puffed up. Lift out with tongs, drain on kitchen paper and set aside. Discard all but 2 tablespoons of the oil.

2 Add the shallots, garlic and ginger to the wok or frying pan and stir-fry for 1 minute. Add the beef and curry paste and stir-fry for a further 3–4 minutes, until tender.

3 Add the beef mixture, the uncooked noodles, soy sauce and fish sauce to the saucepan of stock and simmer for 2–3 minutes, until the noodles have swelled. Serve hot, garnished with the coriander and the reserved crispy noodles.

steak waldorf salad

ingredients

serves 4

2 fillet steaks, about 175 g/
  6 oz each and 2.5-cm/
  1-inch thick
olive or sunflower oil,
  for brushing
pepper
1 tbsp wholegrain mustard
150 ml/5 fl oz mayonnaise
1 tbsp lemon juice
500 g/1 lb 2 oz eating apples
4 celery sticks, thinly sliced
70 g/2½ oz walnut halves,
  broken into pieces
100 g/3½ oz mixed salad leaves
crusty bread, to serve

method

1 Heat a thick, cast-iron griddle pan or heavy-based
  frying pan over a medium heat. Brush each steak with
  oil and season to taste with pepper. When hot, add
  the steaks to the pan, and cook 2½ minutes each
  side for rare, 4 minutes each side for medium and
  6 minutes each side for well done. Remove from the
  pan and reserve.

2 Meanwhile, stir the mustard into the mayonnaise.
  Put the lemon juice into a large bowl. Peel and core
  the apples, then cut them into small chunks and
  immediately toss them in the lemon juice. Stir in the
  mustard mayonnaise. Add the celery and walnuts to
  the apples and toss together.

3 Arrange the salad leaves on 4 plates, then divide
  the apple mixture between them. Very thinly slice
  the steaks, arrange on top of the salad and serve
  immediately with crusty bread.

meatball sandwich

ingredients

serves 4

450 g/1 lb fresh beef mince
1 small onion, grated
2 garlic cloves, crushed
25 g/1 oz fine white breadcrumbs
1 tsp hot chilli sauce
salt and pepper
wholemeal flour, for dusting
groundnut oil, for shallow frying

sandwich

1 tbsp olive oil
1 small onion, sliced
4 sub rolls or small baguettes
4 tbsp mayonnaise
55 g/2 oz sliced jalapeño chillies
    (from a jar)
2 tbsp squeezy mustard

method

1 Place the beef, onion, garlic, breadcrumbs and chilli sauce into a bowl. Season to taste and mix thoroughly. Shape the mixture into 20 small equal-sized balls using floured hands. Cover and chill for 10 minutes or until required.

2 Heat a shallow depth of oil in a wok or heavy-based frying pan until very hot, then fry the meatballs in batches for 6–8 minutes, turning often, until golden brown and firm. Drain on kitchen paper and keep hot.

3 To make the sandwich, heat the olive oil in a clean pan and fry the onion on a moderate heat, stirring occasionally, until soft and golden brown.

4 Split the rolls lengthways and spread with mayonnaise. Arrange the onions, meatballs and jalapeños over the bottom half, squeeze the mustard over and top with the other half. Serve the rolls immediately.

mustard steak sandwiches

ingredients

serves 4

8 slices thick white or brown
    bread
butter, for spreading
2 handfuls mixed salad leaves
3 tbsp olive oil
2 onions, thinly sliced
675 g/1 lb 8 oz rump or sirloin
    steak, about 2.5 cm/
    1 inch thick
1 tbsp Worcestershire sauce
2 tbsp wholegrain mustard
2 tbsp water
salt and pepper

method

1 Spread each slice of bread with some butter and add
   a few salad leaves to the bottom slices.

2 Heat 2 tablespoons of the oil in a large, heavy-based
   frying pan over a medium heat. Add the onions and
   cook, stirring occasionally, for 10–15 minutes until
   softened and golden brown. Using a slotted spoon,
   transfer to a plate and set aside.

3 Increase the heat to high and add the remaining oil
   to the pan. Add the steak, season with pepper to taste
   and cook quickly on both sides to seal. Reduce the
   heat to medium and cook for 2½ minutes each side for
   rare, 4 minutes each side for medium and 6 minutes
   each side for well done. Transfer the steak to the plate
   with the onions.

4 Add the Worcestershire sauce, mustard and water to
   the pan and stir to deglaze by scraping any sediment
   from the base of the pan. Return the onions to the pan,
   season with salt and pepper to taste and mix well.

5 Thinly slice the steak across the grain, divide it between
   the 4 bottom halves of bread and cover with the
   onions. Cover with the top halves of bread and press
   down gently. Serve immediately.

beef teriyaki burgers

ingredients

serves 4

450 g/1 lb fresh best steak
    mince
8 spring onions
2–4 garlic cloves
2.5-cm/1-inch piece fresh
    ginger, grated
½ tsp wasabi or freshly grated
    horseradish, or to taste
4 tsp teriyaki sauce or marinade
2 tsp peanut oil
115 g/4 oz carrot, grated
115 g/4 oz pak choi, shredded
55 g/2 oz cucumber, shredded
4 burger buns
chopped parsley, to garnish

method

1 Place the steak mince, spring onions, garlic, ginger, wasabi and 3 teaspoons of the teriyaki sauce in a food processor and, using the pulse button, blend together. Shape into 4 equal-sized burgers, then cover and leave to chill for 30 minutes.

2 Heat a heavy-based frying pan and add 1 teaspoon of the oil. When hot, add the burgers and cook over a medium heat for 3–5 minutes on each side or according to personal preference. Keep warm.

3 Heat a wok and when really hot, add the remaining oil. Add the carrots and stir-fry for 1 minute, then add the pak choi, cucumber and the remaining teriyaki sauce and stir-fry for a further 1–2 minutes, or until cooked but still crunchy. Spoon the hot salad into the burger buns and top with the burgers. Sprinkle with chopped parsley and serve.

the ultimate cheeseburger

ingredients

serves 4

450 g/1 lb fresh steak mince
4 onions
2–4 garlic cloves, crushed
2–3 tsp grated fresh horseradish
   or 1–1½ tbsp creamed
   horseradish
pepper
8 lean back bacon rashers
2 tbsp sunflower oil
4 slices Cheddar cheese
4 burger buns
shredded lettuce, to serve

method

1 Place the steak mince in a large bowl. Finely grate one of the onions and add to the steak mince in the bowl.

2 Add the garlic, horseradish and pepper to the steak mixture in the bowl. Mix together, then shape into 4 equal-sized burgers. Wrap each burger in 2 rashers of bacon, then cover and leave to chill for 30 minutes.

3 Preheat the grill to medium–high. Slice the remaining onions. Heat the oil in a frying pan. Add the onions and cook over a medium heat for 8–10 minutes, stirring frequently, until the onions are golden brown. Drain on kitchen paper and keep warm.

4 Cook the burgers under the hot grill for 3–5 minutes on each side or until cooked to personal preference. Spoon the onions on top of each burger and top with the cheese slices. Grill until the cheese melts. Serve the burgers on shredded lettuce in burger buns.

classic beef fajitas

ingredients

serves 4–6

700 g/1 lb 9 oz beef skirt steak,
    cut into strips
6 garlic cloves, chopped
juice of 1 lime
large pinch of mild chilli powder
large pinch of paprika
large pinch of ground cumin
1–2 tbsp extra virgin olive oil
12 flour tortillas
butter, for greasing
vegetable oil, for frying
1–2 avocados, stoned, sliced and
    tossed with lime juice
125 ml/4 fl oz soured cream
salt and pepper

salsa

8 ripe tomatoes, diced
3 spring onions, sliced
1–2 fresh green chillies, such as
    jalapeño or serrano, deseeded
    and chopped
3–4 tbsp chopped fresh coriander
5–8 radishes, diced
ground cumin

method

1 Combine the beef with the garlic, lime juice, chilli powder, paprika, cumin and olive oil. Add salt and pepper, mix well and leave to marinate for at least 30 minutes at room temperature, or overnight in the refrigerator.

2 To make the salsa, place the tomatoes in a bowl with the spring onions, green chillies, coriander and radishes. Season to taste with cumin, and salt and pepper. Reserve.

3 Heat the tortillas one by one in a lightly greased non-stick frying pan, wrapping each in foil as you work, to keep it warm.

4 Heat a little oil in a large, heavy-based frying pan over a high heat. Add the meat and stir-fry until browned and just cooked through.

5 Serve the sizzling hot meat with the warm tortillas, the salsa, avocado and soured cream for each person to make their own fajitas.

steak with country gravy

ingredients

serves 4

4 rump steaks, about 140 g/
5 oz each
125 g/4½ oz plain flour
pinch of cayenne pepper,
or to taste
3–4 tbsp rendered bacon fat or
sunflower or groundnut oil
300 ml/10 fl oz full-fat milk
or single cream
salt and pepper
deep-fried okra, to serve

method

1 Put the steaks between pieces of greaseproof paper and use a rolling pin to beat them until they are about 5-mm/¼-inch thick. Set aside. Put the flour onto a large plate and season with cayenne pepper and salt and pepper to taste. Dust the steaks with the seasoned flour on both sides, shaking off any excess, and reserve the leftover flour.

2 Heat 3 tablespoons of the bacon fat in a large frying pan over a medium–high heat. Add as many steaks as will fit without overcrowding the pan and cook until they are cooked through and are crisp and brown on the outside. Transfer the steaks to a plate and keep warm in a low oven while cooking the remaining steaks, if necessary. Add more fat to the pan as needed.

3 For the country gravy, put 5 tablespoons of the reserved seasoned flour into a small bowl, slowly stir in half the milk then stir until no lumps remain.

4 Pour off all but about 1 tablespoon of the fat in the frying pan. Pour the milk mixture into the pan, stirring to scrape up the sediment. Pour in the remaining milk and bring to the boil. Reduce the heat and simmer for 2 minutes, stirring constantly, to remove the raw flour taste. Taste and adjust the seasoning, if necessary. Serve the steaks with deep-fried okra and the gravy.

steak & kidney pie

ingredients

serves 4–6

filling

900 g/2 lb stewing steak, trimmed
    of excess fat and cut into
    2.5-cm/1-inch cubes
225 g/8 oz lambs' kidneys,
    cored and chopped
2 tbsp plain flour
2 tsp dried mixed herbs
55 g/2 oz butter
1 onion, thinly sliced
300 ml/10 fl oz beef stock
1 tbsp Worcestershire sauce
300 g/10½ oz ready-made
    shortcrust pastry, chilled
1 egg, beaten
salt and pepper
cooked peas, to serve

method

1 Mix together the steak, kidneys, flour and herbs and
   season. Melt half the butter in a large pan. Cook
   the onion over a low heat, stirring occasionally, for
   5 minutes. Add the remaining butter and the meat
   mixture. Increase the heat and cook, stirring frequently,
   for 10 minutes. Pour in the stock and Worcestershire
   sauce and season. Bring to the boil, reduce the heat,
   cover and simmer, stirring occasionally, for 1½–2 hours,
   until tender. Transfer to a large pie dish and leave to cool.

2 Preheat the oven to 230°C/450°F/Gas Mark 8. Remove
   the pastry from the refrigerator and roll out on a
   floured surface to 2.5 cm/1 inch larger than the top
   of the dish. Cut out a 15-mm/⅝-inch strip all the way
   around. Brush the rim of the dish with water and
   press the strip on to it. Brush with water and lift the
   remaining pastry on top. Trim off the excess and crimp
   the edges to seal. Make a slit in the centre and brush
   with beaten egg. Roll out the trimmings and use to
   decorate the pie, then brush with beaten egg.

3 Bake for 10 minutes, then brush the pie with beaten
   egg. Reduce the oven temperature to 180°C/350°F/
   Gas Mark 4 and bake for a further 20 minutes, until the
   pastry is golden brown. Serve immediately with peas.

steak & chips with herb butter

ingredients

serves 4

2 tbsp chopped fresh parsley

2 tbsp chopped fresh thyme

85 g/3 oz unsalted butter, softened

4 sirloin steaks, about 225 g/8 oz each

salt and pepper

oven chips

450 g/1 lb potatoes, peeled

2 tbsp sunflower oil

method

1 To make the chips, preheat the oven to 200°C/400°F/ Gas Mark 6. Cut the potatoes into thick, even-sized chips. Rinse them under cold running water and then dry well on a clean tea towel. Place in a bowl, add the oil and toss together until coated.

2 Spread the chips on a baking sheet and cook in the preheated oven for 40–45 minutes, turning once, until golden.

3 Place the butter in a small bowl and beat in the chopped parsley and thyme with a fork until fully incorporated. Cover with clingfilm and leave to chill in the refrigerator until required.

4 Preheat a griddle pan to high. Season the steaks with salt and pepper to taste.

5 Cook the steaks on the preheated griddle for 2½ minutes each side for rare, 4 minutes each side for medium and 6 minutes each side for well done. Transfer to serving plates and serve immediately, topped with the herb butter and accompanied by the chips.

pepper steak

ingredients

serves 4

2 tbsp black or mixed dried
    peppercorns, coarsely crushed
4 fillets steaks, about
    2.5-cm/1-inch thick,
    at room temperature
15 g/½ oz butter
1 tsp sunflower oil
4 tbsp brandy
4 tbsp crème fraîche or
    double cream (optional)
salt and pepper
watercress leaves, to garnish
chips, to serve

method

1 Spread out the crushed peppercorns on a plate and
    press the steaks into them to coat on both sides.

2 Melt the butter with the oil in a large sauté or frying
    pan over a medium–high heat. Add the steaks in a
    single layer and cook for 2½ minutes each side for rare,
    4 minutes each side for medium and 6 minutes each
    side for well done.

3 Transfer the steaks to a warmed plate and set aside,
    covering with foil to keep warm. Pour the brandy into
    the pan to deglaze, increase the heat and use a
    wooden spoon to scrape any sediment from the base
    of the pan. Continue boiling until reduced to around
    2 tablespoons.

4 Stir in any accumulated juices from the steaks. Spoon
    in the crème fraîche, if using, and continue boiling
    until the sauce is reduced by half again. Taste, and
    adjust the seasoning if necessary. Spoon the pan sauce
    over the steaks, garnish with the watercress and serve
    at once with chips.

tabasco steaks with watercress butter

ingredients

serves 4

1 bunch of watercress
85 g/3 oz unsalted butter,
    softened
4 sirloin steaks, about
    225 g/8 oz each
4 tsp Tabasco sauce
oil, for brushing
salt and pepper

method

1 Using a sharp knife, finely chop enough watercress to fill 4 tablespoons. Reserve a few watercress leaves for the garnish. Place the butter in a small bowl and beat in the chopped watercress with a fork until fully incorporated. Cover with clingfilm and leave to chill in the refrigerator until required.

2 Sprinkle each steak with 1 teaspoon of the Tabasco sauce, rubbing it in well. Season to taste with salt and pepper.

3 Heat a ridged, cast-iron griddle pan over a medium heat and brush lightly with oil. Season the steaks to taste with salt and pepper, add to the griddle pan and cook for 2½ minutes each side for rare, 4 minutes each side for medium and 6 minutes each side for well done. Transfer to serving plates, garnish with the reserved watercress leaves and serve immediately, topped with the watercress butter.

griddled steak with hot chilli salsa

ingredients

serves 4

sunflower oil, for brushing
4 sirloin steaks, about
    225 g/8 oz each
salt and pepper

hot chilli salsa

4 fresh red habanero or Scotch
    bonnet chillies
4 fresh green poblano chillies
3 tomatoes, peeled, deseeded
    and diced
2 tbsp chopped fresh coriander
1 tbsp red wine vinegar
2 tbsp olive oil
salt
a few leaves of lamb's lettuce,
    to garnish

method

1 For the salsa, preheat the grill to high. Arrange the chillies on a baking sheet. Cook under the preheated grill, turning frequently, until blackened and charred. Leave to cool. When cool enough to handle, peel off the skins. Halve and deseed the chillies, then finely chop the flesh.

2 Mix the chillies, tomatoes and coriander together in a bowl. Whisk the vinegar and oil together in a jug, season to taste with salt and pour over the salsa. Toss well, cover and chill in the refrigerator until required.

3 Heat a ridged, cast-iron griddle pan over a medium heat and brush lightly with oil. Season the steaks to taste with salt and pepper, add to the griddle pan and cook for 2½ minutes each side for rare, 4 minutes each side for medium and 6 minutes each side for well done. Serve immediately with the salsa, garnished with a few leaves of lamb's lettuce.

prime rib of beef

ingredients

serves 2 per rib

4 kg/9 lb prime rib of beef roast
(4 to 7 ribs, trimmed
and tied)
butter (about ½ tbsp per rib)
salt and pepper

sauce

6 tbsp creamed horseradish sauce
6 tbsp soured cream

method

1 Place the prime rib in a large, sturdy metal roasting pan (no rack is needed as bones form a natural rack). Rub the entire surface of the roast with butter, and season very generously with salt and pepper. Leave the prime rib at room temperature for 2 hours. Preheat the oven to 230°C/450°F/Gas Mark 8.

2 Put the roast in the preheated oven for 20 minutes to sear the outside. Turn the oven down to 160°C/325°F/Gas Mark 3 and roast, allowing 15 minutes per 450 g/1 lb of meat.

3 Transfer to a serving platter, and let the prime rib rest, loosely covered with foil in a warm place, for at least 30 minutes before slicing and serving. Carving the meat too early will cause the juice to be lost.

4 In a small bowl mix the horseradish sauce and soured cream together and serve with the beef.

beef pot roast with potatoes & dill

ingredients

serves 6

2½ tbsp plain flour
1 tsp salt
¼ tsp pepper
1 rolled brisket joint, weighing
    1.6 kg/3 lb 8 oz
2 tbsp vegetable oil
2 tbsp butter
1 onion, finely chopped
2 celery stalks, diced
2 carrots, peeled and diced
1 tsp dill seed
1 tsp dried thyme or oregano
350 ml/12 fl oz red wine
225 ml/8 fl oz beef stock
4–5 potatoes, cut into large
    chunks and boiled until
    just tender
2 tbsp chopped fresh dill, to serve

method

1 Preheat the oven to 140°C/275°F/Gas Mark 1.

2 Mix 2 tablespoons of the flour with the salt and pepper in a shallow dish. Dip the meat to coat. Heat the oil in an ovenproof casserole and brown the meat all over. Transfer to a plate.

3 Add half the butter to the casserole and cook the onion, celery, carrots, dill seed and thyme for 5 minutes. Return the meat and juices to the casserole.

4 Pour in the wine and enough stock to reach one-third of the way up the meat. Bring to the boil, cover and cook in the oven for 3 hours, turning the meat every 30 minutes. After it has been cooking for 2 hours, add the potatoes and more stock if necessary.

5 When ready, transfer the meat and vegetables to a warmed serving dish. Strain the cooking liquid into a pan.

6 Mix the remaining butter and flour to a paste. Bring the cooking liquid to the boil. Whisk in small pieces of the flour and butter paste, whisking constantly until the sauce is smooth. Pour the sauce over the meat and vegetables. Sprinkle with the fresh dill to serve.

beef en daube
with mustard mash

ingredients

serves 2

2 tsp vegetable oil

225 g/8 oz extra lean braising
    steak, cut into 8 pieces

10 small shallots, peeled and
    left whole

1 garlic clove, peeled and crushed

1 medium tomato, chopped

100 g/3½ oz mushrooms,
    finely sliced

150 ml/¼ pint red wine

100 ml/3½ fl oz chicken stock

1 small bouquet garni

1 tsp cornflour, mixed with a
    little water into a paste

salt and pepper

mustard mash

2 medium floury potatoes, peeled
    and sliced

1½–2 tbsp skimmed milk, heated

1 tsp Dijon mustard, to taste

method

1 Preheat the oven to 180°C/350°F/Gas Mark 4.

2 Heat the oil in a heavy-based flameproof casserole.
   Add the meat and shallots and cook over a high heat,
   stirring, for 4–5 minutes to brown the meat on all sides.
   Add the garlic, tomato, mushrooms, wine and stock,
   and tuck the bouquet garni in well.

3 Bring to a simmer on the hob, cover and transfer to the
   oven to cook for 45–60 minutes, or until everything is
   tender. About 30 minutes before the beef is ready,
   place the potatoes in boiling water and simmer for
   20 minutes or until just tender. Remove from heat,
   drain well and put in a bowl. Add the milk and mash
   well. Stir in the mustard to taste, and keep warm.

4 Use a slotted spoon to transfer the meat and
   vegetables to a warmed serving dish and keep warm.
   Cook the sauce on the hob over a high heat until
   reduced by half. Reduce the heat, remove the bouquet
   garni and check the seasoning.

5 Add the cornflour to the sauce, stirring well, and bring
   back to a simmer. Pour the sauce over the meat and
   serve with the mustard mash.

beef wellington

ingredients

serves 6

2 tbsp olive or vegetable oil
1.5 kg/3 lb 5 oz beef fillet,
    cut from the middle of the
    fillet, trimmed of fat and sinew
55 g/2 oz butter
150 g/5½ oz mushrooms, chopped
2 garlic cloves, crushed
150 g/5½ oz smooth liver pâté
1 tbsp finely chopped fresh parsley
2 tsp English mustard
500 g/1 lb 2 oz ready-made
    puff pastry
1 egg, lightly beaten
salt and pepper
wilted greens and roasted root
    vegetables, to serve

method

1 Place a large frying pan over a high heat and add the
   oil. Rub salt and pepper to taste into the beef and sear
   very quickly all over in the pan. Set aside to cool.

2 Heat the butter in the frying pan over a medium heat,
   add the mushrooms and fry for 5 minutes. Reduce the
   heat, add the garlic and fry for another 5 minutes. Put
   the mushrooms and garlic in a bowl, add the pâté and
   parsley, and beat with a fork. Leave to cool.

3 Preheat the oven to 220°C/425°F/Gas Mark 7. Rub the
   mustard over the seared beef fillet. Roll out the pastry
   into a rectangle large enough to wrap the whole fillet
   with some to spare. Spread the mushroom paste in
   the middle of the pastry in a shape the size of the base
   of the beef and lay the beef on top. Brush the edges of
   the pastry with beaten egg and fold it over, edges
   overlapping, and across the meat to enclose it.

4 Place the pastry-wrapped beef in a roasting tin with
   the join underneath and brush with beaten egg. Leave
   to chill in the refrigerator for 15 minutes, then transfer
   to the preheated oven and bake for 50 minutes. Check
   after 30 minutes – if the pastry looks golden brown,
   cover it in foil to prevent it burning.

5 Serve the beef immediately with wilted greens and
   roasted root vegetables.

chilli con carne

ingredients

serves 6

4 tbsp sunflower oil
2 onions, chopped
1 garlic clove, chopped
1 tbsp plain flour
900 g/2 lb braising steak, diced
300 ml/10 fl oz beef stock
300 ml/10 fl oz red wine
2–3 fresh red chillies, deseeded and chopped
800 g/1 lb 12 oz canned red kidney beans, drained and rinsed
400 g/14 oz canned chopped tomatoes
salt and pepper
tortilla chips, to serve

method

1 Heat half of the oil in a heavy-based saucepan. Add half the chopped onion and the garlic and cook, stirring occasionally, for 5 minutes, until softened. Remove with a slotted spoon.

2 Place the flour on a plate and season well with salt and pepper, then toss the meat in the flour to coat. Cook the meat in the pan, in batches, until browned all over, then return the meat and the onion mixture to the saucepan. Pour in the stock and wine and bring to the boil, stirring. Reduce the heat and simmer for 1 hour.

3 Meanwhile, heat the remaining oil in a frying pan. Add the remaining onion and the chillies and cook, stirring occasionally, for 5 minutes. Add the beans and tomatoes with their juice and break up with a wooden spoon. Simmer for 25 minutes, until thickened.

4 Divide the meat between individual plates, top with the bean mixture and serve with tortilla chips.

variation

For a richer flavour, add 55 g/2 oz melted dark chocolate and 2 heaped teaspoons of cocoa powder to the chilli just before serving and stir in well.

beef & ale pie

ingredients

serves 4–6

900 g/2 lb stewing steak, trimmed
    of excess fat and cut into
    2.5-cm/1-inch cubes
4 tbsp plain flour
1 tsp dried thyme
115 g/4 oz butter
2 onions, thinly sliced
2 carrots, thinly sliced
140 g/5 oz mushrooms,
    thinly sliced
500 ml/18 fl oz beef stock
400 ml/14 fl oz brown
    ale or stout
300 g/10½ oz ready-made
    shortcrust pastry, chilled
1 egg, beaten
salt and pepper

method

1 Mix together the steak, flour, thyme and a pinch each of salt and pepper. Melt the butter in a large pan, add the meat and cook over a medium heat, stirring frequently, for 10 minutes, until browned. Add the onions, carrots and mushrooms, pour in the stock and ale and bring to the boil. Reduce the heat, cover and simmer, stirring occasionally, for 1½–2 hours, until the meat is tender. Season and transfer the mixture to a large pie dish. Leave to cool.

2 Preheat the oven to 200°C/400°F/Gas Mark 6. Remove the pastry from the refrigerator and roll out the pastry on a floured surface to 2.5 cm/1 inch larger than the top of the dish. Cut out a 15-mm/⅝-inch strip all the way around. Brush the rim of the dish with water and press the strip on to it. Brush with water and lift the remaining dough on top. Trim off the excess and crimp the edges to seal. Make a small slit in the centre and brush with beaten egg. Roll out the trimmings and use to decorate the pie, then brush with beaten egg.

3 Bake for 35–40 minutes, until golden brown. Serve the pie immediately.

braised veal in red wine

ingredients

serves 6

25 g/1 oz plain flour
900 g/2 lb stewing veal or
    beef, cubed
4 tbsp olive oil
350 g/12 oz button onions
2 garlic cloves, finely chopped
350 g/12 oz carrots, sliced
300 ml/10 fl oz full-bodied
    red wine
150 ml/5 fl oz beef or chicken
    stock
400 g/14 oz canned chopped
    tomatoes with herbs in juice
pared rind of 1 lemon
1 bay leaf
1 tbsp chopped fresh flat-leaf
    parsley, plus extra to garnish
1 tbsp chopped fresh basil
1 tsp chopped fresh thyme
salt and pepper
boiled rice, to serve

method

1 Preheat the oven to 180°C/350°F/Gas Mark 4. Put the flour and pepper to taste in a polythene bag, add the meat and shake well to coat each piece. Heat the oil in a large, flameproof casserole. Add the meat, in batches, and cook for 5–10 minutes, stirring constantly, until browned all over. Remove with a slotted spoon and set aside.

2 Add the whole onions, garlic and carrots to the casserole and cook, stirring frequently, for 5 minutes until beginning to soften.

3 Return the meat to the casserole. Pour in the wine, scraping any sediment from the base of the casserole, then add the stock, tomatoes with their juice, lemon rind, bay leaf, parsley, basil, thyme and salt and pepper to taste. Bring to the boil, then cover the casserole.

4 Transfer to the preheated oven and cook for 2 hours, or until the meat is tender.

5 Serve hot, garnished with extra chopped parsley and accompanied by boiled rice.

saltimbocca

ingredients

serves 4

4 pieces of veal
4 large, thin slices Parma ham
 or San Daniele ham
4 large sage leaves
100 g/3½ oz unsalted butter
200 ml/7 fl oz Marsala, Madeira
 or dry white wine
salt and pepper
sautéed potatoes and a green
 salad, to serve

method

1 Lay the pieces of veal on a board and flatten them with a mallet or rolling pin until they are the same size as the ham slices. Lay down a piece of ham, put a piece of veal on top and place a sage leaf at the edge nearest to you. Season with salt and pepper then roll the meat around the sage leaf and secure it with a cocktail stick. The ham should be on the outside. Repeat with all 4 pieces.

2 Place a wide, heavy-based saucepan over a high heat. Add the butter and then the meat rolls and brown them quickly on all sides. Add the Marsala and reduce the heat to a simmer. Cover and cook for about 10–15 minutes, until the meat is cooked through. Remove the rolls and keep them warm. Increase the heat to reduce the liquid for 2 minutes to thicken.

3 Serve the rolls on warmed plates with sautéed potatoes and a green salad and pour over a little of the sauce.

lamb & feta cheeseburgers

ingredients

serves 4–6

450 g/1 lb fresh lamb mince

225 g/8 oz feta cheese, crumbled

2 garlic cloves, crushed

6 spring onions, finely chopped

85 g/3 oz ready-to-eat prunes, chopped

25 g/1 oz pine kernels, toasted

55 g/2 oz fresh wholemeal breadcrumbs

1 tbsp chopped fresh rosemary

1 tbsp sunflower oil

salt and pepper

to serve

steamed quinoa

baby spinach leaves

tartare sauce

method

1 Place the lamb mince in a large bowl with the cheese, garlic, spring onions, prunes, pine kernels and fresh fresh breadcrumbs. Mix well, breaking up any lumps of mince.

2 Add the rosemary and salt and pepper to the lamb mixture in the bowl. Mix together, then shape into 4–6 equal-sized burgers. Cover and leave to chill for 30 minutes.

3 Preheat the grill to medium. Place the burgers on a foil-lined grill rack and brush lightly with oil. Cook under the hot grill for 4 minutes before turning over and brushing with the remaining oil. Continue to cook for 4 minutes, or until cooked to personal preference. Serve with quinoa, baby spinach and tartare sauce.

shepherd's pie

ingredients

serves 4

700 g/1 lb 9 oz fresh lean
   lamb mince
2 onions, chopped
225 g/8 oz carrots, diced
1–2 garlic cloves, crushed
1 tbsp plain flour
200 ml/7 fl oz lamb stock
200 g/7 oz canned
   chopped tomatoes
1 tsp Worcestershire sauce
1 tsp chopped fresh sage
1 kg/2 lb 4 oz potatoes
25 g/1 oz margarine
3–4 tbsp skimmed milk
125 g/4½ oz button
   mushrooms (optional)
salt and pepper

method

1 Preheat the oven to 200°C/400°F/Gas Mark 6. Place the
   lamb mince in a heavy-based saucepan with no extra
   fat and cook gently until the meat begins to brown.

2 Add the onions, carrots and garlic and continue to
   cook gently for 10 minutes. Stir in the plain flour and
   cook for about 1–2 minutes, then gradually stir in the
   stock and chopped tomatoes and bring to the boil.

3 Add the Worcestershire sauce and sage and season to
   taste with salt and pepper. Cover and simmer gently
   for 25 minutes, giving an occasional stir.

4 Meanwhile, cook the potatoes in boiling salted water
   until tender, then drain thoroughly and mash, beating
   in the margarine and enough milk to give a stiff
   consistency. Season to taste with salt and pepper.

5 Slice the mushrooms, if using, stir into the meat, then
   taste and adjust the seasoning if necessary. Turn into
   a shallow ovenproof dish.

6 Spread the potatoes evenly over the meat. Cook in the
   preheated oven for 30 minutes, or until piping hot and
   the potato is golden brown.

moussaka

ingredients

serves 4

2 aubergines, thinly sliced
450 g/1 lb fresh lean lamb mince
2 onions, thinly sliced
1 tsp finely chopped garlic
400 g/14 oz canned tomatoes
2 tbsp chopped fresh parsley
2 eggs
300 ml/10 fl oz low-fat
  natural yogurt
1 tbsp freshly grated
  Parmesan cheese
salt and pepper

method

1 Preheat the oven to 180°C/350°F/Gas Mark 4. Dry-fry the aubergine slices, in batches, in a non-stick frying pan on both sides until browned. Remove from the pan.

2 Add the lamb mince to the frying pan and cook for 5 minutes, stirring, until browned. Stir in the onions and garlic and cook for 5 minutes, or until browned. Add the tomatoes, parsley and salt and pepper, then bring to the boil and simmer for 20 minutes, or until the meat is tender.

3 Arrange half the aubergine slices in a layer in an ovenproof dish. Add the meat mixture, then a final layer of the remaining aubergine slices.

4 Beat the eggs in a bowl, then beat in the yogurt and add salt and pepper to taste. Pour the mixture over the aubergines and sprinkle the grated cheese on top. Bake the moussaka in the oven for 45 minutes, or until golden brown. Serve straight from the dish.

lamb with aubergine

ingredients

serves 4

1 aubergine
4–8 lamb chops
3 tbsp olive oil
1 onion, roughly chopped
1 garlic clove, finely chopped
400 g/14 oz canned chopped
     tomatoes in juice
pinch of sugar
16 black olives, stoned and
     roughly chopped
1 tsp chopped fresh herbs such
     as basil, flat-leaf parsley
     or oregano
salt and pepper

method

1 Cut the aubergine into 2-cm/³/₄-inch cubes, put in a colander standing over a large plate, and sprinkle each layer with salt. Cover with a plate and place a heavy weight on top. Leave for 30 minutes.

2 Preheat the grill. Rinse the aubergine cubes under cold running water, then pat dry with kitchen paper. Season the lamb chops with pepper.

3 Place the lamb chops on the grill pan and cook under a medium heat for 10–15 minutes until tender, turning once during the cooking time.

4 Meanwhile, heat the olive oil in a saucepan, add the aubergine, onion and garlic and fry for 10 minutes, until softened and starting to brown. Add the tomatoes and their juice, the sugar, olives, chopped herbs, salt and pepper and simmer for 5–10 minutes.

5 To serve, spoon the sauce onto 4 warmed serving plates and top with the lamb chops.

lancashire hotpot

ingredients

serves 4–6

900 g/2 lb best end lamb chops
3 lambs' kidneys
55 g/2 oz butter
900 g/2 lb floury potatoes, such as
    King Edwards or Maris Piper,
    peeled and sliced
3 onions, halved and finely sliced
2 tsp fresh thyme leaves
1 tsp finely chopped fresh
    rosemary
600 ml/1 pint chicken stock
salt and pepper

method

1 Preheat the oven to 160°C/325°F/Gas Mark 3.

2 Trim the chops of any excess fat. Cut the kidneys in half, remove the core and cut into quarters. Season all the meat well with salt and pepper.

3 Butter a large, shallow ovenproof dish or deep roasting tin with half the butter and arrange a layer of potatoes in the bottom. Layer up the onions and meat, seasoning well with salt and pepper and sprinkling the herbs between each layer. Finish with a neat layer of overlapping potatoes.

4 Pour in most of the stock so that it covers the meat.

5 Melt the remaining butter and brush the top of the potato with it. Reserve any remaining butter. Cover with foil and cook in the oven for 2 hours.

6 Uncover the hotpot and brush the potatoes again with the melted butter.

7 Return the hotpot to the oven and cook for a further 30 minutes, allowing the potatoes to get brown and crisp. You may need to increase the temperature if not browning sufficiently, or place under a hot grill. Serve the hotpot at the table, making sure that everyone gets a good helping of potatoes and the meat.

scotch broth

ingredients

serves 6-8

700 g/1 lb 9 oz neck of lamb
1.7 litres/3 pints water
55 g/2 oz pearl barley
2 onions, chopped
1 garlic clove, finely chopped
3 small turnips, diced
3 carrots, peeled and thinly sliced
2 celery sticks, sliced
2 leeks, sliced
salt and pepper
2 tbsp chopped fresh parsley,
    to garnish

method

1 Cut the meat into small pieces, removing as much fat as possible. Put into a large saucepan and cover with the water. Bring to the boil over a medium heat and skim off any scum that appears.

2 Add the pearl barley, reduce the heat and cook gently, covered, for 1 hour.

3 Add the prepared vegetables and season well with salt and pepper. Continue to cook for a further hour. Remove from the heat and allow to cool slightly.

4 Remove the meat from the saucepan using a slotted spoon and strip the meat from the bones. Discard the bones and any fat or gristle. Place the meat back in the saucepan and leave to cool thoroughly, then refrigerate overnight.

5 Scrape the solidified fat off the surface of the soup. Reheat, season with salt and pepper to taste and serve piping hot, garnished with the parsley scattered over the top.

lamb shanks with roasted onions

ingredients

serves 4

4 x 350 g/12 oz lamb shanks,
    with fat removed
6 garlic cloves
2 tbsp virgin olive oil
1 tbsp very finely chopped
    fresh rosemary
4 red onions, tops cut off
350 g/12 oz carrots, cut into
    thin batons
4 tbsp water
salt and pepper

method

1 Preheat the oven to 180°C/350°F/Gas Mark 4. Using a small, sharp knife, make 6 incisions in each shank. Cut the garlic cloves lengthways into 4 slices. Insert 6 garlic slices in the incisions in each lamb shank. Place the lamb in a roasting tin, drizzle with the olive oil, sprinkle with the rosemary and season with pepper. Roast in the preheated oven for 45 minutes.

2 Wrap each of the onions in a square of foil. Remove the roasting tin from the oven and season the lamb shanks with salt. Return the tin to the oven and place the wrapped onions on the shelf next to it. Roast for a further 1–1¼ hours, until the lamb is very tender. Meanwhile, bring a large saucepan of water to the boil. Add the carrot batons and blanch for 1 minute. Drain and refresh under cold water.

3 Remove the roasting tin from the oven when the lamb is meltingly tender and transfer it to a warmed serving dish. Skim off any fat from the roasting tin and place it over a medium heat. Add the carrots and cook for 2 minutes, then add the water, bring to the boil and simmer, stirring constantly and scraping up the glazed bits from the base of the roasting tin. Transfer the carrots and sauce to the serving dish. Remove the onions from the oven and unwrap. Cut off the tops, and add to the serving dish. Serve immediately.

rack of lamb

ingredients

serves 2

1 trimmed rack of lamb (about
    250–300 g/9–10½ oz)
1 garlic clove, crushed
150 ml/5 fl oz red wine
1 fresh rosemary sprig, crushed
    to release the flavour
1 tbsp olive oil
150 ml/5 fl oz lamb stock
2 tbsp redcurrant jelly
salt and pepper

mint sauce

small bunch of fresh mint
    leaves, chopped
2 tsp caster sugar
2 tbsp boiling water
2 tbsp white wine vinegar

method

1 Place the rack of lamb in a non-metallic bowl and rub
  all over with the garlic. Pour over the wine and place
  the rosemary sprig on top. Cover and leave to marinate
  in the refrigerator for 3 hours, or overnight if possible.

2 To make the mint sauce, combine the mint leaves with
  the sugar in a small bowl. Add the boiling water and
  stir to dissolve the sugar. Add the wine vinegar and leave
  to stand for 30 minutes before serving with the lamb.

3 Preheat the oven to 220°C/425°F/Gas Mark 7.

4 Remove the lamb from the marinade, reserving the
  marinade, dry the meat with kitchen paper and season
  well with salt and pepper. Place in a small roasting tin,
  drizzle with the oil and roast in the oven for 15–20
  minutes, depending on how well done you like your
  lamb. Remove the lamb from the oven and leave to
  rest, covered with foil, in a warm place for 5 minutes.

5 Meanwhile, place the marinade in a small pan, bring
  to the boil over a medium heat and bubble away for
  2–3 minutes. Add the lamb stock and redcurrant jelly
  and simmer until a syrupy consistency is achieved.

6 Carve the lamb into cutlets and serve on warmed
  plates with the redcurrant jelly sauce spooned over
  the top. Serve the mint sauce separately.

roast lamb with garlic & rosemary

ingredients

serves 6

1 leg of lamb, weighing
1.5 kg/3 lb 5 oz
6 garlic cloves, thinly sliced
lengthways
8 fresh rosemary sprigs
4 tbsp olive oil
salt and pepper

glaze

4 tbsp redcurrant jelly
300 ml/10 fl oz rosé wine

method

1 Preheat the oven to 200°C/400°F/Gas Mark 6. Using a small knife, cut slits all over the leg of lamb. Insert 1–2 garlic slices and 4–5 rosemary needles in each slit. Place any remaining rosemary in the base of a roasting tin. Season the lamb to taste with salt and pepper and place in the roasting tin. Pour over the oil. Cover with foil and roast for 1 hour 20 minutes.

2 Mix the redcurrant jelly and wine together in a small saucepan. Heat gently, stirring constantly, until combined. Bring to the boil, then reduce the heat and simmer until reduced. Remove the lamb from the oven and pour over the glaze. Return to the oven and cook uncovered for about 10 minutes, depending on how well done you like it.

3 Remove the lamb from the roasting tin, tent with foil and leave to rest for 15 minutes in a warm place before carving and serving.

poultry

smoked chicken & cranberry salad

ingredients

serves 4

1 smoked chicken, weighing
    1.3 kg/3 lb
115 g/4 oz dried cranberries
2 tbsp apple juice or water
200 g/7 oz sugar snap peas
2 ripe avocados
juice of ½ lemon
4 lettuce hearts
1 bunch of watercress, trimmed
55 g/2 oz rocket
55 g/2 oz walnuts, chopped,
    to garnish (optional)

dressing

2 tbsp olive oil
1 tbsp walnut oil
2 tbsp lemon juice
1 tbsp chopped fresh mixed
    herbs, such as parsley
    and lemon thyme
salt and pepper

method

1 Carve the chicken carefully, slicing the white meat.
   Divide the legs into thighs and drumsticks and trim
   the wings. Cover with clingfilm and refrigerate.

2 Put the cranberries in a bowl. Stir in the apple juice,
   cover with clingfilm and leave to soak for 30 minutes.

3 Meanwhile, blanch the sugar snap peas, refresh under
   cold running water and drain.

4 Peel, stone and slice the avocados, then toss in the
   lemon juice to prevent browning.

5 Separate the lettuce hearts and arrange on a large
   serving platter with the avocados, sugar snap peas,
   watercress, rocket and chicken.

6 Put all the dressing ingredients, with salt and pepper
   to taste, in a screw-top jar, screw on the lid and shake
   until well blended. Drain the cranberries and mix them
   with the dressing, then pour over the salad.

7 Serve immediately, scattered with walnuts if you are
   using them.

chicken caesar salad

ingredients

serves 6

3 tbsp sunflower oil
2 thick slices of white bread, cubed
3 skinless, boneless chicken
    breasts, about 140 g/5 oz each
2 small heads of cos lettuce,
    roughly chopped
2 tbsp Parmesan cheese shavings
salt and pepper

dressing

1 garlic clove, crushed
2 canned anchovy fillets, drained
    and finely chopped
5 tbsp light olive oil
2 tbsp white wine vinegar
2 tbsp mayonnaise
2 tbsp freshly grated Parmesan
    cheese
salt and pepper

method

1 Preheat the oven to 200°C/400°F/Gas Mark 6. Place
   2 tablespoons of the sunflower oil in a bowl, add the
   bread and toss to coat in the oil. Spread out on a
   baking sheet, season well with salt and pepper and
   bake in the preheated oven for 10 minutes, until crisp
   and golden brown.

2 Meanwhile, brush the chicken breasts with the
   remaining sunflower oil and season to taste with salt
   and pepper. Cook on a preheated cast-iron griddle for
   8–10 minutes on each side, until the chicken is tender
   and the juices run clear when a skewer is inserted into
   the thickest part of the meat.

3 To make the dressing, place all the ingredients in a
   small bowl and mix together thoroughly until smooth
   and creamy.

4 Slice the hot cooked chicken and toss lightly with
   the lettuce and croutons. Divide the salad among
   4 serving bowls and drizzle over the dressing. Scatter
   over the Parmesan cheese shavings and serve the
   salad immediately.

chicken noodle soup

ingredients

serves 4–6

2 skinless, boneless chicken
    breasts
1.2 litres/2 pints chicken stock
3 carrots, peeled and sliced into
    5-mm/¼-inch slices
85 g/3 oz vermicelli
    (or other small noodles)
salt and pepper
fresh tarragon leaves,
    to garnish

method

1 Place the chicken breasts in a large saucepan, add the
   stock and bring to a simmer. Cook for 25–30 minutes.
   Skim any foam from the surface if necessary. Remove
   the chicken from the stock and keep warm.

2 Continue to simmer the stock, add the carrots and
   vermicelli and cook for 4–5 minutes.

3 Thinly slice or shred the chicken breasts and place
   in warmed serving dishes.

4 Season the soup to taste with salt and pepper and
   pour over the chicken. Serve at once garnished with
   the tarragon.

chicken liver pâté

ingredients

serves 4

140 g/5 oz butter
1 onion, finely chopped
1 garlic clove, finely chopped
250 g/9 oz chicken livers
½ tsp Dijon mustard
2 tbsp brandy (optional)
salt and pepper
brown toast fingers, to serve

method

1 Melt half the butter in a large frying pan over a medium heat. Add the onion and cook, stirring frequently, for 3–4 minutes until softened but not browned. Add the garlic and cook, stirring, for 2 minutes.

2 Check the chicken livers and remove any discoloured parts using a pair of scissors. Add the livers to the frying pan and cook over a medium–high heat, stirring frequently, for 5–6 minutes until browned all over.

3 Season well with salt and pepper and stir in the mustard and brandy, if using.

4 Transfer the chicken liver mixture to a food processor and process until smooth. Add the remaining butter, cut into small pieces, and process again until creamy.

5 Press the pâté into a serving dish or 4 small ramekins, smooth the surface and cover. Store in the refrigerator. To keep for more than 2 days, seal the surface by pouring over a little clarified butter and leaving to set. Serve the pâté with brown toast fingers.

chicken nuggets

ingredients

serves 4

3 skinless, boneless chicken breasts
4 tbsp wholemeal plain flour
1 tbsp wheatgerm
½ tsp ground cumin
½ tsp ground coriander
1 egg, lightly beaten
2 tbsp olive oil

dipping sauce

100 g/3½ oz sun-blush tomatoes
100 g/3½ oz fresh tomatoes, peeled, deseeded and chopped
2 tbsp mayonnaise
pepper

method

1 Preheat the oven to 190°C/375°F/Gas Mark 5. Cut the chicken breasts into 4-cm/1½-inch chunks. Mix the flour, wheatgerm, cumin, coriander, and pepper to taste, in a bowl, then divide in half and put on 2 separate plates. Put the beaten egg on a third plate.

2 Pour the oil into a baking tray and heat in the oven. Roll the chicken pieces in one plate of flour, shake to remove any excess, then roll in the egg and in the second plate of flour, again shaking off any excess flour. When all the nuggets are ready, remove the baking tray from the oven and toss the nuggets in the hot oil. Roast in the oven for 25–30 minutes until golden and crisp.

3 Meanwhile, to make the dipping sauce, put both kinds of tomatoes in a blender or food processor and process until smooth. Add the mayonnaise and process again until well combined.

4 Remove the nuggets from the oven and drain on kitchen paper. Serve with the dipping sauce.

bacon-wrapped chicken burgers

ingredients

serves 4

450 g/1 lb fresh chicken mince
1 onion, grated
2 garlic cloves, crushed
55 g/2 oz pine kernels, toasted
55 g/2 oz Gruyère cheese, grated
2 tbsp fresh snipped chives
2 tbsp wholemeal flour
8 slices lean back bacon
1–2 tbsp sunflower oil
salt and pepper

to serve

4 crusty rolls, sliced
sliced red onion
chopped lettuce
mayonnaise
chopped spring onions

method

1 Place the chicken mince, onion, garlic, pine kernels, Gruyère cheese, chives and salt and pepper in a food processor. Using the pulse button, blend the mixture together using short sharp bursts. Scrape out onto a board and shape into 4 even-sized burgers. Coat in the flour, then cover and chill for 1 hour.

2 Wrap each burger with 2 bacon slices, securing in place with a wooden cocktail stick.

3 Heat a heavy-based frying pan and add the oil. When hot, add the burgers and cook over a medium heat for 5–6 minutes on each side, or until thoroughly cooked through.

4 Serve the burgers in the crusty rolls with sliced red onion, chopped lettuce, a spoonful of mayonnaise and chopped spring onions.

chicken & spinach lasagne

ingredients

serves 4

350 g/12 oz frozen chopped
    spinach, thawed and drained
½ tsp freshly grated nutmeg
450 g/1 lb lean, cooked chicken,
    skinned and diced
4 sheets dried no pre-cook
    lasagne verde
1½ tbsp cornflour
425 ml/15 fl oz milk
70 g/2½ oz freshly grated
    Parmesan cheese
salt and pepper

tomato sauce

400 g/14 oz canned chopped
    tomatoes
1 onion, finely chopped
1 garlic clove, crushed
150 ml/5 fl oz white wine
3 tbsp tomato purée
1 tsp dried oregano
salt and pepper

method

1 To make the tomato sauce, put the tomatoes into a
   pan and stir in the onion, garlic, wine, tomato purée
   and oregano. Bring to the boil and simmer for 20
   minutes, until thick. Season well with salt and pepper.

2 Preheat the oven to 190°C/375°F/Gas Mark 5. Drain the
   spinach again and spread it out on kitchen paper to
   make sure that as much water as possible is removed.
   Layer the spinach in the base of a large ovenproof
   baking dish. Sprinkle with nutmeg and season to taste
   with salt and pepper.

3 Arrange the diced chicken over the spinach and spoon
   over the tomato sauce. Arrange the sheets of lasagne
   over the tomato sauce.

4 Blend the cornflour with a little of the milk to make a
   paste. Pour the remaining milk into a pan and stir in
   the paste. Heat, stirring, until the sauce thickens.
   Season well.

5 Spoon the sauce over the lasagne sheets and transfer
   the dish to a baking tray. Sprinkle the grated Parmesan
   cheese over the sauce and bake in the preheated oven
   for 25 minutes until golden, then serve.

buttered chicken parcels

ingredients

serves 4

55 g/2 oz butter
4 shallots, finely chopped
300 g/10½ oz frozen spinach,
    thawed
450 g/1 lb blue cheese, such
    as Stilton, crumbled
1 egg, lightly beaten
1 tbsp snipped fresh chives
1 tbsp chopped fresh oregano
4 skinless, boneless chicken
    breasts
8 slices Parma ham
salt and pepper
baby spinach leaves, to serve
fresh chives, to garnish

method

1 Melt half of the butter in a frying pan over a medium heat. Add the shallots and cook, stirring, for 4 minutes. Remove from the heat and leave to cool for 10 minutes.

2 Preheat the oven to 180°C/350°F/Gas Mark 4. Using your hands, squeeze out as much moisture from the thawed spinach as possible. Transfer the spinach into a large bowl, add the shallots, cheese, egg, herbs and salt and pepper to taste. Mix together well.

3 Halve each chicken breast then put each piece between 2 sheets of clingfilm and pound gently with a rolling pin to flatten to an even thickness. Spoon some cheese mixture into the centre of each piece, then roll it up. Wrap each roll in a slice of Parma ham and secure with a cocktail stick. Transfer to a roasting dish, dot with the remaining butter and bake in the preheated oven for 30 minutes until golden.

4 Divide the baby spinach leaves between 4 serving plates. Remove the chicken from the oven and place 2 chicken rolls on each plate. Garnish with fresh chives and serve.

chicken kiev

ingredients

serves 8

115 g/4 oz butter, softened
3–4 garlic cloves, very finely
    chopped
1 tbsp chopped fresh parsley
1 tbsp snipped fresh chives
finely grated rind and juice
    of ½ lemon
8 skinless, boneless chicken
    breasts, about 115 g/4 oz
    each
55 g/2 oz plain flour
2 eggs, lightly beaten
175 g/6 oz dry breadcrumbs
groundnut or sunflower oil,
    for deep-frying
salt and pepper

method

1 Beat the butter in a bowl with the garlic, herbs, lemon rind and juice. Season to taste with salt and pepper. Divide into 8 pieces, then shape into cylinders. Wrap in foil and chill for about 2 hours, until firm.

2 Place the chicken between 2 sheets of clingfilm. Pound gently with a rolling pin to flatten the chicken to an even thickness. Place a butter cylinder on each chicken piece and roll up. Secure with cocktail sticks.

3 Place the flour, eggs and breadcrumbs in separate shallow dishes. Dip the rolls into the flour, then the egg and, finally, the breadcrumbs. Place on a plate, cover and chill for 1 hour.

4 Heat the oil in a saucepan or deep-fat fryer to 180–190°C/350–375°F, or until a cube of bread browns in 30 seconds. Deep-fry the chicken in batches for 8–10 minutes, or until cooked through and golden brown. Drain on kitchen paper. Serve immediately.

variation

Instead of the butter, garlic, herb and lemon filling, fill the chicken pieces with ham or prosciutto and a slice of goat's cheese.

sherried chicken liver brochettes

ingredients

serves 6

400 g/14 oz chicken livers,
    trimmed
3 rindless streaky bacon rashers
1 ciabatta loaf or small
    French stick, halved
    horizontally
225 g/8 oz baby spinach leaves,
    washed

marinade

150 ml/5 fl oz dry sherry
4 tbsp olive oil
1 tsp wholegrain mustard
salt and pepper

mustard mayonnaise

8 tbsp mayonnaise
1 tsp wholegrain mustard

method

1 Cut the chicken livers into 5-cm/2-inch pieces.
   Combine the ingredients for the marinade in a shallow
   dish. Add the chicken livers and toss to coat in the
   marinade. Cover and leave to marinate in the
   refrigerator for 3–4 hours.

2 Mix the mayonnaise and mustard together in a small
   bowl. Cover with clingfilm and chill in the refrigerator
   until required.

3 Preheat the barbecue. Cut each rasher in half. Put on
   a chopping board and use the back of a knife to
   stretch gently until almost double in length. Remove
   the chicken livers from the marinade, reserving the
   marinade. Wrap the bacon rashers around half of the
   chicken liver pieces. Thread the bacon and chicken liver
   rolls and the plain chicken liver pieces alternately onto
   6 presoaked wooden skewers.

4 Cook over hot coals, turning frequently and brushing
   with the marinade, but not for the last 5 minutes of the
   cooking time, for 10–12 minutes until cooked through.

5 Meanwhile, cut each bread half into 3 pieces and toast
   the cut sides on the barbecue until golden brown.

6 To serve, top the toasted bread with the spinach and
   put the kebabs on top. Spoon over the mayonnaise.

mustard & honey drumsticks

ingredients

serves 4

8 chicken drumsticks
sprigs of fresh parsley,
　to garnish

glaze

125 ml/4 fl oz clear honey
4 tbsp Dijon mustard
4 tbsp wholegrain mustard
4 tbsp white wine vinegar
2 tbsp sunflower oil
salt and pepper

method

1 Using a sharp knife, make 2–3 diagonal slashes in the chicken drumsticks and place them in a large, non-metallic dish.

2 Mix all the ingredients for the glaze together in a jug and season to taste with salt and pepper. Pour the glaze over the drumsticks, turning until the drumsticks are well coated. Cover with clingfilm and leave to marinate in the refrigerator for at least 1 hour.

3 Preheat the grill. Drain the chicken drumsticks, reserving the marinade. Cook the chicken under the preheated grill, turning frequently and brushing with the reserved marinade, for 25–30 minutes, or until thoroughly cooked. Transfer to serving plates, garnish with sprigs of parsley and serve immediately.

chicken burgers

ingredients

serves 4

4 large skinless, boneless
   chicken breasts
1 large egg white
1 tbsp cornflour
1 tbsp plain flour
1 egg, beaten
55 g/2 oz fresh white
   breadcrumbs
2 tbsp sunflower oil
2 beef tomatoes, sliced

to serve

4 burger buns
shredded lettuce
mayonnaise

method

1 Place the chicken breasts between 2 sheets of non-stick
   baking paper and flatten slightly using a meat mallet
   or a rolling pin. Beat the egg white and cornflour
   together, then brush over the chicken. Cover and
   leave to chill for 30 minutes, then coat in the flour.

2 Place the egg and breadcrumbs in 2 separate bowls
   and coat the burgers first in the egg, allowing any
   excess to drip back into the bowl, then in the
   breadcrumbs.

3 Heat a heavy-based frying pan and add the oil. When
   hot, add the burgers and cook over a medium heat for
   6–8 minutes on each side, or until thoroughly cooked.
   If you are in doubt, it is worth cutting one of the
   burgers in half. If there is any sign of pinkness, cook
   for a little longer. Add the tomato slices for the last
   1–2 minutes of the cooking time to heat through.
   Serve in burger buns with lettuce and mayonnaise.

grilled chicken with lemon

ingredients

serves 4

4 chicken quarters
grated rind and juice of
    2 lemons
4 tbsp olive oil
2 garlic cloves, crushed
2 fresh thyme sprigs,
    plus extra to garnish
salt and pepper

method

1 Prick the skin of the chicken quarters all over with a
  fork. Put the chicken in a non-metallic dish, add the
  lemon juice, oil, garlic, thyme and salt and pepper
  to taste and mix together well. Cover and leave to
  marinate in the refrigerator for at least 2 hours.

2 To cook the chicken, preheat the grill to medium.
  Put the chicken in the grill pan and baste with the
  marinade. Cook under the preheated grill, turning
  occasionally and basting with the marinade, but not
  for the last 10 minutes of the cooking time, for 30–40
  minutes until the chicken is tender and the juices run
  clear when a skewer is inserted into the thickest part
  of the meat.

3 Serve hot, garnished with the lemon rind and a few
  thyme sprigs.

paprika chicken

ingredients

serves 4

4 boneless chicken breasts, about
115 g/4 oz each, skin on
150 ml/5 fl oz freshly squeezed
lemon juice
1–1½ tsp mild or hot Spanish
paprika, to taste
about 2 tbsp olive oil
70 g/2½ oz Serrano ham, diced
4 large onions, thinly sliced
125 ml/4 fl oz dry white wine
125 ml/4 fl oz chicken stock
salt and pepper
fresh thyme sprigs, to garnish

method

1 Put the chicken in a non-metallic bowl. Pour over
the lemon juice, cover and leave to marinate in the
refrigerator overnight. Remove the chicken from the
marinade and pat dry with kitchen paper. Rub the skin
with the paprika and salt and pepper to taste.

2 Heat 2 tablespoons oil in a large, heavy-based frying
pan with a lid or flameproof casserole over a medium–
high heat. Add the chicken breasts, skin-side down,
until the skins are crisp and golden. Remove from the
frying pan. Stir in the ham, cover and cook until the fat
runs. Add the onions and cook, stirring occasionally
and adding a little extra oil if necessary, for 5 minutes,
or until the onions are softened but not browned.

3 Add the wine and stock and bring to the boil, stirring.
Return the chicken breasts to the frying pan and
season to taste with salt and pepper. Reduce the heat,
cover and simmer for 20 minutes, or until the chicken
is tender and the juices run clear when a skewer is
inserted into the thickest part of the meat. Bring the
sauce to the boil and cook until the juices have
reduced. Taste and adjust the seasoning.

4 Divide the sauce between 4 individual warmed plates
and arrange a chicken breast on top of each. Garnish
with thyme sprigs and serve immediately.

chicken, sausage & bean stew

ingredients

serves 4

2 tbsp vegetable oil

4 boneless, skinless chicken
breasts, about 115 g/4 oz
each, cubed

225 g/8 oz coarse-textured pork
sausage, cut into large chunks

4 frankfurter sausages, halved

1 onion, finely chopped

3 carrots, thinly sliced

1 garlic clove, very finely chopped

1 tsp dried thyme

¼–½ tsp dried chilli flakes

400 g/14 oz canned
chopped tomatoes in juice

400 g/14 oz canned cannellini
beans, drained and rinsed

150 ml/5 fl oz chicken stock

salt and pepper

chopped fresh flat-leaf parsley,
to garnish

method

1 Heat the oil in a large, heavy-based saucepan over a medium–high heat. Add the chicken, pork sausage and frankfurters and cook until lightly browned all over. Reduce the heat to medium. Add the onion and carrots and cook, stirring frequently, for 5 minutes, or until the vegetables have softened.

2 Stir in the garlic, thyme and chilli flakes and cook, stirring, for 1 minute. Stir in the tomatoes with their juice, beans and stock. Season to taste with salt and pepper. Bring to the boil, then reduce the heat and simmer over a low heat, stirring occasionally, for 20–30 minutes. Garnish with chopped parsley just before serving.

chicken casserole with a herb crust

ingredients

serves 4

4 whole chicken legs, dusted in flour

1 tbsp olive oil

1 tbsp butter

1 onion, chopped

3 garlic cloves, sliced

4 parsnips, peeled and cut into large chunks

150 ml/5 fl oz dry white wine

850 ml/1½ pints chicken stock

3 leeks, white parts only, sliced

85 g/3 oz prunes, halved (optional)

1 tbsp English mustard

1 bouquet garni sachet

100 g/4 oz fresh breadcrumbs

85 g/3 oz Caerphilly cheese, crumbled

50 g/2 oz mixed chopped tarragon and flat-leaf parsley

salt and pepper

method

1 Preheat the oven to 180°C/350°F/Gas Mark 4.

2 Fry the chicken in a casserole with the olive oil and butter, until golden brown. Remove with a slotted spoon and keep warm. Add the onion, garlic and parsnips to the casserole and cook for 20 minutes or until the mixture is golden brown. Add the wine, stock, leeks, prunes, if using, English mustard and bouquet garni. Season with salt and pepper.

3 Add the chicken to the casserole, place on the lid and cook in the oven for 1 hour. Meanwhile mix together the breadcrumbs, cheese and herbs.

4 Remove the casserole from the oven and increase the heat to 200°C/400°F/Gas Mark 6.

5 Remove the lid of the casserole and sprinkle over the breadcrumb mixture. Return to the oven for 10 minutes, uncovered, until the crust starts to brown slightly. Remove from the oven and serve.

chicken & butternut casserole

ingredients

serves 4–6

2 tbsp olive oil
4 skinless, boneless chicken thighs,
    about 100 g/3½ oz each,
    cut into bite-sized pieces
1 large onion, sliced
2 leeks, chopped
2 garlic cloves, chopped
1 butternut squash, peeled,
    deseeded and cut into cubes
2 carrots, diced
400 g/14 oz canned chopped
    tomatoes and herbs
400 g/14 oz canned mixed beans,
    drained and rinsed
100 ml/3½ fl oz vegetable
    or chicken stock, plus extra
    if needed
salt and pepper

method

1 Preheat the oven to 160°C/325°F/Gas Mark 3.

2 Heat half the oil in a large, flameproof casserole over a high heat, add the chicken and cook, turning frequently, for 2–3 minutes until browned all over. Reduce the heat to medium, remove the chicken with a slotted spoon and set aside.

3 Add the remaining oil to the casserole, add the onion and leeks and cook, stirring occasionally, for 10 minutes, or until soft. Add the garlic, squash and carrots and cook, stirring, for 2 minutes. Add the tomatoes and their juice, beans, the chicken pieces and stock, stir well and bring to a simmer.

4 Cover, transfer to the preheated oven and cook for 1–1¼ hours, stirring once or twice – if the casserole looks too dry, add a little extra stock. Season with a very little salt and pepper to taste before serving.

turkey, leek & stilton soup

ingredients

serves 4

55 g/2 oz butter
1 large onion, chopped
1 leek, trimmed and sliced
325 g/11½ oz cooked
    turkey meat, sliced
600 ml/1 pint chicken stock
150 g/5½ oz Stilton cheese,
    crumbled
150 ml/5 fl oz double cream
1 tbsp chopped fresh tarragon
pepper
fresh tarragon leaves and
    croûtons, to garnish

method

1 Melt the butter in a saucepan over a medium heat. Add the onion and cook, stirring, for 4 minutes, until slightly softened. Add the leek and cook for another 3 minutes.

2 Add the turkey to the pan and pour in the stock. Bring to the boil, then reduce the heat and simmer gently, stirring occasionally, for about 15 minutes. Remove from the heat and leave to cool a little.

3 Transfer half of the soup into a food processor and blend until smooth. Return the mixture to the pan with the rest of the soup, stir in the Stilton, cream and tarragon and season with pepper. Reheat gently, stirring. Remove from the heat, ladle into warmed soup bowls, garnish with tarragon and croûtons and serve.

turkey & lentil soup

ingredients

serves 4

1 tbsp olive oil
1 garlic clove, chopped
1 large onion, chopped
200 g/7 oz mushrooms, sliced
1 red pepper, deseeded and
    chopped
6 tomatoes, peeled, deseeded
    and chopped
1.2 litre/2 pints chicken stock
150 ml/5 fl oz red wine
85 g/3 oz cauliflower florets
1 carrot, peeled and chopped
200 g/7 oz red lentils
350 g/12 oz cooked turkey
    meat, chopped
1 courgette, trimmed and
    chopped
1 tbsp shredded fresh basil
salt and pepper
thick slices of fresh crusty bread,
    to serve

method

1 Heat the oil in a large saucepan. Add the garlic and
    onion and cook over a medium heat, stirring, for
    3 minutes, until slightly softened. Add the mushrooms,
    red pepper and tomatoes and cook for a further
    5 minutes, stirring. Pour in the stock and red wine, then
    add the cauliflower, carrot and red lentils. Season with
    salt and pepper. Bring to the boil, then lower the heat
    and simmer the soup gently for 25 minutes, until the
    vegetables are tender and cooked through.

2 Add the turkey and courgette to the pan and cook for
    10 minutes. Stir in the shredded basil and cook for a
    further 5 minutes, then remove from the heat and ladle
    into serving bowls. Serve with fresh crusty bread.

roast turkey with cider sauce

ingredients

serves 8

1 boneless turkey breast roast,
    weighing 1 kg/2 lb 4 oz
1 tbsp corn oil
salt and pepper

filling

25 g/1 oz butter
2 shallots, finely chopped
1 celery stalk, finely chopped
1 cooking apple, peeled, cored
    and diced
80 g/2¾ oz prunes, stoned
    and chopped
55 g/2 oz raisins
3 tbsp chicken stock
4 tbsp cider
1 tbsp chopped fresh parsley

cider sauce

1 shallot, very finely chopped
300 ml/10 fl oz cider
125 ml/4 fl oz chicken stock
1 tsp cider vinegar

method

1 Preheat the oven to 190°C/375°F/Gas Mark 5.

2 To make the filling, melt the butter in a pan. Add the
  shallots and cook, stirring occasionally, for 5 minutes.
  Add the celery and apple and cook for 5 minutes. Add
  the remaining ingredients, cover, and simmer. Transfer
  to a bowl and leave to cool.

3 Place the turkey roast on a chopping board and slice
  almost completely through, from the thin side toward
  the thicker side. Open out, place between 2 sheets of
  clingfilm, and flatten with a rolling pin to an even
  thickness. Season to taste with salt. Spoon on the
  filling, roll the roast around it, and tie with string.

4 Heat the oil in a roasting tin over medium heat, add
  the roast, and brown all over. Transfer to the preheated
  oven and roast for 1 hour 10 minutes, or until cooked
  through and the juices run clear. Remove from the tin
  and cover with foil.

5 For the sauce, pour off any fat from the tin and set over
  medium heat. Add the shallot and half the cider and
  cook for 1–2 minutes, scraping any sediment from the
  bottom of the tin. Add the remaining cider, stock and
  vinegar and cook until reduced and thickened. Remove
  and discard the string from the turkey and cut into
  slices. Serve with the cider sauce.

roast turkey with bread sauce

ingredients

serves 8

4 tbsp ready-made stuffing,
    of your choice
5 kg/11 lb turkey
40 g/1½ oz butter

bread sauce

1 onion, peeled
4 cloves
600 ml/1 pint milk
115 g/4 oz fresh white
    breadcrumbs
55 g/2 oz butter
salt and pepper

to serve

cranberry sauce
cooked vegetables
roasted potatoes

method

1 Preheat the oven to 220°C/425°F/Gas Mark 7. If you
  are planning on stuffing the turkey, spoon the stuffing
  into the neck cavity and close the flap of skin with a
  skewer. If you prefer to cook the stuffing separately,
  simply cook according to the recipe's instructions.

2 Place the bird in a large roasting tin and rub it all over
  with the butter. Roast in the preheated oven for 1 hour,
  then lower the oven temperature to 180°C/350°F/
  Gas Mark 4 and roast for a further 2½ hours.

3 Meanwhile, make the bread sauce. Stud the onion
  with the cloves, then place in a saucepan with the milk,
  breadcrumbs and butter. Bring just to boiling point
  over a low heat, then remove from the heat and leave
  to stand in a warm place to infuse. Just before serving,
  remove the onion and cloves and reheat the sauce
  gently, beating well with a wooden spoon. Season to
  taste with salt and pepper.

4 Check that the turkey is cooked by inserting a skewer
  or the point of a sharp knife into the thigh – if the
  juices run clear, it is ready. Transfer the bird to a carving
  board, cover loosely with foil and leave to rest.

5 Carve the turkey and serve with the warm bread sauce,
  stuffing, cranberry sauce, vegetables and potatoes.

turkey ciabatta with walnuts

ingredients

serves 2

2 ciabatta rolls
115 g/4 oz blue cheese, such as
    Stilton or Danish blue, finely
    diced or crumbled
115 g/4 oz walnuts, chopped
8 large fresh sage leaves, finely
    shredded
4 slices cooked turkey breast
seedless green grapes,
    to serve

method

1 Preheat the grill to a medium–high setting. Slice the
   ciabatta rolls in half horizontally and toast the cut sides
   on the rack in the grill pan. Remove the top halves.
   Turn the bottom halves over and toast the undersides
   until brown and crisp. When the breads are toasted,
   set them aside and reduce the heat to a low setting.

2 Meanwhile, mix the blue cheese, walnuts and sage.
   Lay 2 turkey slices on the base of each roll and top with
   the cheese and walnut mixture, piling it up in the
   middle. Cover with the top of the roll.

3 Heat the rolls under the grill, well away from the heat,
   for 3–4 minutes, until the breads are hot and the
   cheese is beginning to melt. Increase the heat slightly,
   if necessary, to medium but do not turn it up high
   enough to brown the tops of the rolls before they are
   warmed through.

4 Serve the hot turkey ciabatta rolls with green grapes as
   an accompaniment.

lemon & mint turkey burgers

ingredients

serves 6

500 g/1 lb 2 oz fresh turkey
    mince
½ small onion, grated
finely grated rind and juice
    of 1 small lemon
1 garlic clove, finely chopped
2 tbsp finely chopped
    fresh mint
½ tsp pepper
1 tsp sea salt
1 egg, beaten
1 tbsp olive oil, plus extra
    for frying
lemon wedges, to serve

method

1 Place all the ingredients in a bowl and mix well with
a fork. Shape the mixture into 12 balls, rolling them
with the palm of your hand. Flatten into rounds about
2 cm/¾ inch thick. Cover and leave in the refrigerator
for at least 1 hour, or overnight.

2 Heat about 5 tablespoons of oil in a large heavy-based
frying pan. When the oil starts to look hazy, add the
burgers, cooking in batches if necessary. Cook over a
medium–high heat for 4–5 minutes on each side, until
golden brown and cooked through.

3 Drain the burgers on kitchen paper and transfer to a
warmed serving dish. Serve with lemon wedges.

turkey & mushroom pie

ingredients

serves 6

55 g/2 oz butter
2 tbsp plain flour, plus extra
    for dusting
225 ml/8 fl oz chicken stock
3 tbsp double cream
1 onion, chopped
2 carrots, sliced
2 celery sticks, chopped
55 g/2 oz mushrooms, sliced
450 g/1 lb cooked turkey, diced
55 g/2 oz frozen peas
350 g/12 oz ready-made
    shortcrust pastry, chilled
1 egg, lightly beaten
salt and pepper

method

1 Melt half the butter in a saucepan over a medium heat, stir in the flour and cook, stirring constantly, for 1 minute. Gradually whisk in the stock and bring to the boil, whisking constantly. Reduce the heat and simmer for 2 minutes, then stir in the cream. Season to taste.

2 Melt the remaining butter in a large frying pan over a low heat. Add the onion and carrots and cook, stirring occasionally, for 5 minutes, or until softened. Add the celery and mushrooms and cook, stirring occasionally, for 5 minutes, then stir in the turkey and peas. Stir into the cream sauce, then transfer to a large pie dish.

3 Preheat the oven to 190°C/375°F/Gas Mark 5. Remove the pastry from the refrigerator and roll out on a lightly floured surface to 2.5 cm/1 inch larger than the top of the dish. Cut out a 15-mm/⁵∕₈-inch strip all the way around. Brush the rim of the dish with water and press the strip on to it. Brush with water and lift the pastry on top. Trim off the excess and crimp the edges to seal. Make a slit in the centre and brush with beaten egg. Roll out the trimmings and use to decorate the pie, then brush with beaten egg. Bake for 40 minutes, until golden. Serve immediately.

turkey & potato pie

ingredients

serves 4

300 g/10½ oz waxy potatoes,
    cubed
25 g/1 oz butter
1 tbsp vegetable oil
300 g/10½ oz lean turkey
    meat, diced
1 red onion, halved and sliced
2 tbsp plain flour, plus extra
    for dusting
300 ml/10 fl oz milk
150 ml/5 fl oz double cream
2 celery stalks, sliced
75 g/2¾ oz dried apricots,
    chopped
25 g/1 oz walnut pieces
2 tbsp chopped fresh parsley
350 g/12 oz ready-made
    shortcrust pastry, chilled
1 egg, lightly beaten
salt and pepper

method

1 Place the potatoes in a saucepan of boiling water and
    cook for 10 minutes, until tender. Drain and set aside.

2 Meanwhile, heat the butter and oil in a heavy-based
    saucepan. Add the diced turkey and cook over
    medium heat, stirring frequently, for 5 minutes, until
    golden brown.

3 Add the sliced onion and cook for 2–3 minutes. Stir
    in the flour and cook, stirring constantly, for 1 minute.
    Gradually stir in the milk and cream. Bring to the boil,
    stirring, then lower the heat to a simmer.

4 Stir in the celery, apricots, walnut pieces, parsley
    and potatoes. Season to taste. Spoon the potato
    and turkey mixture into the base of a large pie dish
    and leave to cool.

5 Preheat the oven to 200°C/400°F/Gas Mark 6. On a
    lightly floured surface, roll out the pastry to 2.5 cm/
    1 inch larger than the dish. Cut out a 15-mm/⅝-in strip
    and place it on the dampened rim of the dish. Brush
    with water and cover with the pastry lid. Brush the
    top of the pie with beaten egg and bake for 25–30
    minutes, or until golden brown. Serve immediately.

peking duck

ingredients

serves 4

1.8 kg/4 lb duck
1.8 litres/3¼ pints boiling water
4 tbsp clear honey
2 tsp dark soy sauce
carrot strips, to garnish

sauce

2 tbsp sesame oil
125 ml/4 fl oz hoisin sauce
125 g/4½ oz caster sugar
125 ml/4 fl oz water

to serve

Chinese pancakes
cucumber matchsticks
shredded spring onions

method

1 Place the duck on a rack set over a roasting tin and pour 1.2 litres/2 pints of the boiling water over it. Remove the duck and rack and discard the water. Pat dry with clean kitchen paper, replace the duck and rack, cover and reserve for several hours.

2 Mix the honey, 600 ml/1 pint of boiling water and soy sauce together. Brush the mixture as a glaze over the skin and inside the duck. Reserve the remaining glaze. After 1 hour, coat the duck with another layer of glaze. Leave to dry and repeat until all of the glaze is used.

3 Preheat the oven to 190°C/375°F/Gas Mark 5. For the sauce, heat the oil in a saucepan. Add the hoisin sauce, sugar and water. Simmer for 2–3 minutes, until thickened. Cool and chill until required.

4 Cook the duck in the preheated oven for 30 minutes. Turn the duck over and cook for 20 minutes. Turn the duck again and cook for 20–30 minutes, or until the meat is cooked through and the skin is crisp.

5 Remove the duck from the oven and leave to stand for 10 minutes. Heat the Chinese pancakes in a bamboo steamer for 5–7 minutes. Cut the duck into strips and divide between the serving plates. Garnish with carrot strips and serve with the pancakes, cucumber matchsticks, shredded spring onions and sauce.

duck breasts with chilli & lime

ingredients

serves 4

4 boneless duck breasts
1 tsp vegetable oil
125 ml/4 fl oz chicken stock
2 tbsp plum jam
salt and pepper
lime wedges and freshly cooked
    rice, to serve

marinade

2 garlic cloves, crushed
4 tsp light soft brown sugar
3 tbsp lime juice
1 tbsp soy sauce
1 tsp chilli sauce

method

1 To make the marinade, mix the garlic, sugar, lime juice, and the soy and chilli sauces together.

2 Using a small sharp knife, cut deep slashes in the skin of the duck breasts to make a diamond pattern. Place the duck breasts in a wide, non-metallic dish.

3 Spoon the marinade over the duck breasts, turning to coat them evenly in the mixture. Cover the dish with clingfilm and leave to marinate in the refrigerator for at least 3 hours, or overnight if possible.

4 Drain the duck, reserving the marinade. Heat a large, heavy-based frying pan until very hot and brush with the oil. Add the duck breasts, skin-side down, and cook for 4–5 minutes until the skin is browned and crisp. Pour off the excess fat.

5 Turn the duck breasts and cook on the other side for 2–3 minutes to brown. Add the reserved marinade, and the stock and jam and simmer for 2 minutes. Adjust the seasoning to taste. Transfer the duck breasts to serving plates and spoon the juices over. Serve with lime wedges and freshly cooked rice.

roast duck with apple

ingredients

serves 4

4 duck portions, about
    350 g/12 oz each
4 tbsp dark soy sauce
2 tbsp light muscovado sugar
2 red-skinned apples
2 green-skinned apples
juice of 1 lemon
2 tbsp clear honey
a few bay leaves
salt and pepper
assorted freshly cooked
    vegetables, to serve

apricot sauce

400 g/14 oz canned apricots
    in fruit juice
4 tbsp sweet sherry

method

1 Preheat the oven to 190°C/375°F/Gas Mark 5. Wash the duck and trim away any excess fat. Place on a wire rack over a roasting tin and prick all over with a fork.

2 Brush the duck with the soy sauce. Sprinkle over the sugar and season with pepper. Cook in the preheated oven, basting occasionally, for 50–60 minutes, or until the meat is cooked through and the juices run clear when a skewer is inserted into the thickest part of the meat.

3 Meanwhile, core the apples and cut each into 6 wedges then place in a small bowl and mix with the lemon juice and honey. Transfer to a small roasting tin, add a few bay leaves and season to taste with salt and pepper. Cook alongside the duck, basting occasionally, for 20–25 minutes until tender. Discard the bay leaves.

4 To make the sauce, place the apricots in a food processor with the can juices and the sherry. Process until smooth. Alternatively, mash the apricots with a fork until smooth and mix with the juice and sherry.

5 Just before serving, heat the apricot sauce in a small saucepan. Pat the flesh of the duck with kitchen paper to absorb any fat. Serve the duck with the apple wedges, apricot sauce and freshly cooked vegetables.

pork & bacon

bacon butties with home-made tomato sauce

ingredients

serves 2

4 smoked bacon rashers
30 g/1 oz butter, softened
4 slices thick white or brown
   bread
salt and pepper

tomato sauce

2 tbsp olive oil
1 red onion, peeled and chopped
2 garlic cloves, chopped
250 g/9 oz plum tomatoes,
   chopped
250 g/9 oz canned chopped
   tomatoes
$\frac{1}{2}$ tsp ground ginger
$\frac{1}{2}$ tsp chilli powder
40 g/1$\frac{1}{2}$ oz dark brown sugar
100 ml/3$\frac{1}{2}$ fl oz red wine vinegar

method

1 To make the tomato sauce, heat the olive oil in a large saucepan and add the onion, garlic and tomatoes. Add the ginger and chilli and season with salt and pepper to taste. Cook for 15 minutes, or until soft.

2 Pour the mixture into a food processor and blend well. Sieve thoroughly to remove all the seeds. Return the mixture to the pan and add the sugar and vinegar. Return to the boil and cook until it is the consistency of ketchup.

3 Bottle the sauce quickly in sterilized bottles or jars and store in a cool place or refrigerator until required.

4 Preheat the grill to high. Place the rashers of bacon under the hot grill and grill, turning frequently until the bacon is crisp and golden brown. Spread the butter over the slices of bread.

5 Place 2 rashers on the base pieces of bread, season with pepper to taste and spoon or pour some tomato sauce over the bacon. Top with the other slice of bread and serve the butties immediately.

bacon & lentil soup

ingredients

serves 4

450 g/1 lb thick, rindless smoked
  bacon rashers, diced
1 onion, chopped
2 carrots, sliced
2 celery sticks, chopped
1 turnip, chopped
1 large potato, chopped
85 g/3 oz Puy lentils
1 bouquet garni sachet
1 litre/1¾ pints chicken stock
salt and pepper

method

1 Heat a large, heavy-based saucepan or flameproof
casserole. Add the bacon and cook over a medium
heat, stirring, for 4–5 minutes, or until the fat runs. Add
the chopped onion, carrots, celery, turnip and potato
and cook, stirring frequently, for 5 minutes.

2 Add the lentils and bouquet garni and pour in the
stock. Bring to the boil, reduce the heat and simmer
for 1 hour, or until the lentils are tender.

3 Remove and discard the bouquet garni and season the
soup to taste with pepper, and with salt, if necessary.
Remove the soup from the heat, ladle into warmed
bowls and serve.

polenta with parma ham

ingredients

serves 3–6

600 ml/1 pint water
70 g/2½ oz quick-cook polenta
25 g/1 oz freshly grated
    Parmesan cheese
25 g/1 oz butter, softened
salt and pepper
2 tbsp extra virgin olive oil,
    plus extra to serve

topping

6 slices Parma ham
85 g/3 oz fontina cheese,
    cut into 6 slices
12 fresh sage leaves

method

1 Line a 15- x 25-cm/6- x 10-inch Swiss roll tin with
   baking paper and set aside. Pour the water into a large
   saucepan and bring to the boil. Reduce the heat so
   that it is just simmering and add a large pinch of salt.
   Add the polenta, stirring constantly. Simmer, stirring
   constantly, for 5 minutes, or until thickened.

2 Remove from the heat and stir in the Parmesan cheese
   and butter and season to taste with pepper. Spoon the
   polenta evenly into the prepared tin and smooth the
   surface with a palette knife. Set aside to cool completely.

3 Preheat the grill to high. Oil a baking sheet and a
   7.5-cm/3-inch plain, round pastry cutter. Turn out the
   polenta onto a work surface, stamp out 6 rounds and
   put on the baking sheet. Brush generously with some
   of the oil and season to taste with salt and pepper.

4 Cook under the preheated grill for 3–4 minutes. Turn
   the rounds over, brush with more of the oil and cook
   for a further 3–4 minutes until golden. Cool completely
   then drape a slice of ham on each round and top with
   a slice of fontina cheese. Brush the sage leaves with the
   remaining oil and put 2 on each round.

5 Cook the polenta rounds under the preheated grill for
   3–4 minutes until the cheese has melted and the sage
   is crisp. Serve immediately, with extra oil for dipping.

pot-roast pork

ingredients

serves 4

1 tbsp sunflower oil
55 g/2 oz butter
1 kg/2 lb 4 oz boned and rolled
    pork loin joint
4 shallots, chopped
6 juniper berries
2 fresh thyme sprigs, plus
    extra to garnish
150 ml/5 fl oz dry cider
150 ml/5 fl oz chicken
    stock
8 celery sticks, chopped
2 tbsp plain flour
150 ml/5 fl oz double cream
salt and pepper

method

1 Heat the oil with half the butter in a large, heavy-based saucepan or flameproof casserole. Add the pork and cook over a medium heat, turning frequently, for 5–10 minutes, or until browned. Transfer to a plate.

2 Add the shallots to the saucepan and cook, stirring frequently, for 5 minutes, or until softened. Add the juniper berries and thyme sprigs and return the pork to the saucepan, with any juices that have collected on the plate. Pour in the cider and stock, season to taste with salt and pepper, then cover and simmer for 30 minutes. Turn the pork over and add the celery. Re-cover the pan and cook for a further 40 minutes.

3 Meanwhile, make a beurre manié by mashing the remaining butter with the flour in a small bowl. Transfer the pork and celery to a platter with a slotted spoon and keep warm. Remove and discard the juniper berries and thyme. Whisk the beurre manié, a little at a time, into the simmering cooking liquid. Cook, stirring constantly, for 2 minutes, then stir in the cream and bring to the boil.

4 Slice the pork and spoon a little of the sauce over it. Garnish with the thyme sprigs and serve immediately. Hand around the remaining sauce separately.

roast pork with crackling

ingredients

serves 4

2 lb 4 oz/1 kg pork loin joint,
boned and the rind
removed and reserved
2 tbsp mustard
salt and pepper
apple sauce, to serve

gravy

1 tbsp flour
300 ml/10 fl oz cider, apple juice,
or chicken stock

method

1 Preheat the oven to 200°C/400°F/Gas Mark 6.

2 Score the pork rind thoroughly with a sharp knife and
sprinkle with salt. Place it on a wire rack on a baking
sheet and roast in the oven for 30–40 minutes until
the crackling is golden brown and crisp.

3 Season the pork well with salt and pepper and spread
the mustard all over. Place in a roasting tin and roast
in the centre of the oven for 20 minutes. Reduce the
oven temperature to 190°C/375°F/Gas Mark 5 and
cook for an additional 50–60 minutes, until the meat is
a good colour and the juices run clear when pierced
with a skewer. Remove the meat from the oven and
place on a warmed serving plate, cover with foil, and
let stand in a warm place.

4 To make the gravy, pour off most of the fat from the
roasting tin, leaving the meat juices and the sediment.
Place the tin over a low heat. Sprinkle in the flour,
whisking well. Cook the paste for a couple of minutes,
then add the cider a little at a time until you have
a smooth gravy. Boil for 2–3 minutes until it is the
required consistency. Season well with salt and
pepper and pour into a warmed serving jug.

5 Carve the pork into slices and serve on warmed plates
with pieces of the crackling, the gravy and apple sauce.

roast ham

ingredients

serves 6

1.3 kg/3 lb boneless
    gammon joint
2 tbsp Dijon mustard
85 g/3 oz brown sugar
½ tsp ground cinnamon
½ tsp ground ginger
18 whole cloves

sauce

2 Seville oranges, halved
4 tbsp redcurrant jelly
4 tbsp port
1 tsp mustard
salt and pepper

method

1 Place the joint in a large pan, cover with cold water,
   and gradually bring to the boil over low heat. Cover
   and simmer gently for 1 hour. Preheat the oven
   to 200°C/400°F/Gas Mark 6.

2 Remove the gammon from the pan and drain. Remove
   the rind from the gammon and discard. Score the fat
   into a diamond-shaped pattern with a sharp knife.

3 Spread the mustard over the fat. Mix the sugar and
   ground spices together on a plate and roll the ham
   in it, pressing down to coat evenly.

4 Stud the diamond shapes with cloves and place the
   joint in a roasting tin. Roast in the oven for 20 minutes
   until the glaze is a rich golden colour. To serve hot,
   cover with foil and leave to stand for 20 minutes
   before carving. If the ham is to be served cold, it can
   be cooked a day ahead.

5 To make the sauce, remove the zest of the oranges
   using a citrus zester. Place the redcurrant jelly, port and
   mustard in a small pan and heat gently until the jelly
   has melted. Squeeze the juice from the oranges into
   the pan. Add the orange zest and season to taste with
   salt and pepper. Serve the sauce cold with the ham.
   The sauce can be kept in a screw-top jar in the
   refrigerator for up to 2 weeks.

spicy meatball risotto

ingredients

serves 4

1 thick slice white bread,
    crusts removed
water or milk, for soaking
450 g/1 lb fresh pork mince
2 garlic cloves, finely chopped
1 tbsp finely chopped onion
1 tsp black peppercorns,
    lightly crushed
pinch of salt
1 egg
corn oil, for shallow-frying
400 g/14 oz canned
    tomatoes, chopped
1 tbsp tomato purée
1 tsp dried oregano
1 tsp fennel seeds
pinch of sugar
1 litre/1¾ pints beef stock
1 tbsp olive oil
40 g/1½ oz butter
1 small onion, finely chopped
280 g/10 oz risotto rice
salt and pepper
fresh basil leaves, to garnish

method

1 Place the bread into a bowl, add the water and leave
to soak for 5 minutes. Squeeze out the water and place
into a dry bowl together with the minced pork, garlic,
onion, crushed peppercorns and salt. Add the egg and
mix thoroughly. Shape the mixture into 12 balls.

2 Heat the corn oil in a frying pan over a medium heat.
Add the meatballs and cook through. Remove and
drain. Combine the tomatoes, tomato purée, herbs and
sugar in a saucepan. Add the meatballs and bring to
the boil. Reduce the heat and simmer for 30 minutes.

3 Bring the stock to the boil in a saucepan, then reduce
the heat and keep simmering gently over a low heat
while you are cooking the risotto. To do this, heat the
olive oil with 25 g/1 oz of the butter in a deep saucepan
until the butter has melted. Stir in the onion and cook
for 5 minutes, until golden. Stir in the rice and red wine.
Gradually add the simmering stock, stirring constantly
after each addition. Increase the heat so that the liquid
bubbles. Cook for 20 minutes. Season to taste.

4 Lift out the cooked meatballs and add to the risotto.
Remove the risotto from the heat and add the
remaining butter. Mix well. Arrange the risotto and a
few meatballs on 4 serving plates. Drizzle with the
tomato sauce, garnish with the basil and serve.

pork with mixed green beans

ingredients

serves 4

2 tbsp vegetable or
    groundnut oil
2 shallots, chopped
225 g/8 oz pork fillet,
    thinly sliced
2.5-cm/1-inch piece fresh
    galangal or ginger, thinly sliced
2 garlic cloves, chopped
300 ml/10 fl oz chicken stock
4 tbsp chilli sauce
4 tbsp crunchy peanut butter
115 g/4 oz fine French beans
115 g/4 oz frozen broad beans
115 g/4 oz runner beans, sliced
crispy noodles, to serve

method

1 Heat the oil in a preheated wok or large frying pan over
a high heat. Add the shallots, pork, galangal and garlic
and stir-fry for 3–4 minutes until the pork is lightly
browned all over.

2 Add the stock, chilli sauce and peanut butter and cook,
stirring, until the peanut butter has melted. Add all the
beans, stir well and simmer for 3–4 minutes, or until
tender and the pork is cooked through. Serve
immediately with crispy noodles.

griddled pork with orange sauce

ingredients

serves 4

4 tbsp freshly squeezed
orange juice
4 tbsp red wine vinegar
2 garlic cloves, finely chopped
4 pork steaks, trimmed of all
visible fat
olive oil, for brushing
pepper

gremolata

3 tbsp finely chopped fresh parsley
zest of 1 lime
zest of ½ lemon
1 garlic clove, very finely chopped

method

1 Mix the orange juice, vinegar and garlic together in
a shallow, non-metallic dish and season to taste with
pepper. Add the pork and turn to coat in the marinade
Cover and leave to marinate in the refrigerator for up
to 3 hours.

2 Meanwhile, mix all the ingredients for the gremolata
together in a small bowl, cover and leave to chill.

3 Heat a non-stick griddle pan over a medium–high
heat and brush lightly with oil. Remove the pork from
the marinade, reserving the marinade. Add the pork to
the griddle pan and cook for 5 minutes on each side,
or until cooked through.

4 Meanwhile, pour the marinade into a small saucepan,
bring to the boil and boil for 5 minutes, or until the
sauce is slightly thickened.

5 Transfer the pork to a serving dish, pour the orange
sauce over and sprinkle with the gremolata. Serve the
pork immediately.

pork chops with peppers

ingredients

serves 4

1 tbsp sunflower oil
4 pork chops, trimmed of
    visible fat
1 onion, chopped
1 garlic clove, finely chopped
1 green pepper, deseeded
    and sliced
1 red pepper, deseeded and sliced
325 g/11½ oz canned
    sweetcorn kernels
1 tbsp chopped fresh parsley
salt and pepper
mashed potatoes, to serve

method

1 Heat the oil in a large, flameproof casserole. Add the pork chops in batches and cook over a medium heat, turning occasionally, for 5 minutes, or until browned. Transfer the chops to a plate with a slotted spoon.

2 Add the chopped onion to the casserole and cook, stirring occasionally, for 5 minutes, or until softened. Add the garlic and peppers and cook, stirring occasionally for a further 5 minutes. Stir in the sweetcorn kernels and their juices, the parsley, and season to taste with salt and pepper.

3 Return the chops to the casserole, spooning the vegetable mixture over them. Cover and simmer for 30 minutes, or until tender. Serve immediately with mashed potatoes.

spareribs in a sweet-and-sour sauce

ingredients

serves 4

450 g/1 lb spareribs, cut into
    bite-sized pieces
vegetable or groundnut oil,
    for deep-frying

marinade

2 tsp light soy sauce
½ tsp salt
pinch of white pepper

sauce

3 tbsp white rice vinegar
2 tbsp sugar
1 tbsp light soy sauce
1 tbsp tomato ketchup
1½ tbsp vegetable or
    groundnut oil
1 green pepper, deseeded
    and roughly chopped
1 small onion, roughly chopped
1 small carrot, finely sliced
½ tsp finely chopped garlic
½ tsp finely chopped ginger
100 g/3½ oz pineapple chunks

method

1 Combine the marinade ingredients in a bowl with
   the spareribs and marinate for at least 20 minutes.

2 Heat enough oil for deep-frying in a wok, deep-fat
   fryer or large heavy-based saucepan until it reaches
   180–190°C/350–375°F, or until a cube of bread browns
   in 30 seconds. Deep-fry the spareribs for 8 minutes.
   Drain and set aside.

3 To prepare the sauce, first mix together the vinegar,
   sugar, light soy sauce and ketchup. Set aside.

4 In a preheated wok or deep pan, heat 1 tablespoon
   of the oil and stir-fry the pepper, onion and carrot for
   2 minutes. Remove and set aside.

5 In the clean preheated wok or deep pan, heat the
   remaining oil and stir-fry the garlic and ginger until
   fragrant. Add the vinegar mixture. Bring back to
   the boil and add the pineapple chunks. Finally, add
   the spareribs and the pepper, onion and carrot. Stir
   until warmed through and serve immediately.

ham & potato pie

ingredients

serves 4–6

filling

225 g/8 oz waxy potatoes, cubed
25 g/1 oz butter
8 shallots, halved
225 g/8 oz smoked ham, cubed
2½ tbsp plain flour
300 ml/10 fl oz milk
2 tbsp wholegrain mustard
50 g/1¾ oz pineapple, cubed
salt and pepper

cheese pastry

225 g/8 oz plain flour, plus extra for dusting
½ tsp mustard powder
pinch of salt
pinch of cayenne pepper
150 g/5½ oz butter
125 g/4½ oz mature Cheddar cheese, grated
2 egg yolks
4–6 tsp iced water
1 egg, lightly beaten

method

1 Cook the potatoes in a saucepan of boiling water for 10 minutes. Drain and set aside.

2 Meanwhile, melt the butter in a separate saucepan over a low heat. Add the shallots and cook, stirring frequently, for 3–4 minutes until beginning to brown.

3 Add the ham and cook, stirring, for 2–3 minutes. Stir in the flour and cook, stirring, for 1 minute. Gradually stir in the milk. Add the mustard and pineapple and bring to the boil, stirring. Season well and add the potatoes.

4 To make the pastry, sift the flour, mustard powder, salt and cayenne pepper into a bowl. Add the butter and cut into the flour, then rub in with your fingertips until the mixture resembles breadcrumbs. Stir in the cheese. Add the egg yolks and water and mix to a smooth dough, adding more water if necessary. Shape into a ball, cover and chill in the refrigerator for 30 minutes.

5 Preheat the oven to 190°C/375°F/Gas Mark 5. Cut the pastry dough in half, roll out one half on a lightly floured surface and use to line a large pie dish. Spoon the filling into the pie dish. Brush the edges with water. Roll out the remaining pastry and press it on top of the pie, sealing the edges. Decorate with the trimmings. Brush with beaten egg and bake in the preheated oven for 40–45 minutes. Serve immediately.

chorizo & pork pie

ingredients

serves 4-6

filling

3 tbsp olive oil
1 onion, finely chopped
2 garlic cloves, finely chopped
280 g/10 oz fresh pork mince
280 g/10 oz chorizo sausage,
    finely chopped
55 g/2 oz stoned black olives,
    finely chopped
4 tbsp full-bodied red wine
4 tbsp sun-dried tomato purée
150 ml/5 fl oz chicken stock

pastry

375 g/13 oz plain flour,
    plus extra for dusting
pinch of salt
300 g/10½ oz butter, diced
about 6 tbsp iced water
1 egg, lightly beaten

method

1 Heat the oil in a large pan. Add the onion and garlic and cook over a low heat, stirring occasionally, for 5 minutes, until softened. Add the pork, increase the heat and cook, stirring frequently, for 5–8 minutes, until evenly browned. Stir in the chorizo, olives, wine, tomato purée and stock and bring to the boil. Reduce the heat, cover and simmer, stirring occasionally, for 25 minutes. Remove from the heat and leave to cool.

2 Meanwhile, make the pastry. Sift the flour with the salt into a bowl and add the butter and water. Mix to a firm but slightly lumpy dough, adding more iced water if necessary. Roll out into a rectangle on a lightly floured surface, then fold the top third down and the bottom third up. Give the dough a quarter turn, roll out and fold again. Repeat once more, then wrap and chill for 30 minutes.

3 Preheat the oven to 200°C/400°F/Gas Mark 6. Cut the pastry into 2 pieces, 1 larger than the other. Roll out the larger piece on a floured surface and use to line a Swiss roll tin. Spoon the filling into the pastry case and brush the rim with beaten egg. Roll out the remaining dough and put it on top. Trim off the excess and crimp the edges to seal. Make a small slit in the centre and brush with beaten egg. Bake for 25–30 minutes, until golden brown. Serve immediately.

red curry pork

ingredients

serves 4

2 tbsp vegetable or groundnut
 oil
1 onion, roughly chopped
2 garlic cloves, chopped
450 g/1 lb pork fillet, thickly
 sliced
1 red pepper, deseeded and cut
 into squares
175 g/6 oz mushrooms, quartered
2 tbsp Thai red curry paste
115 g/4 oz creamed coconut,
 chopped
300 ml/$\frac{1}{2}$ pint vegetable stock
2 tbsp Thai soy sauce
4 tomatoes, peeled, deseeded
 and chopped
handful of fresh coriander,
 chopped
cooked noodles or rice, to serve

method

1 Heat the oil in a wok or large frying pan and fry the
 onion and garlic for 1–2 minutes, until they are
 softened but not browned.

2 Add the pork slices and stir-fry for 2–3 minutes until
 browned all over. Add the pepper, mushrooms and
 curry paste.

3 Dissolve the coconut in the stock and add to the wok
 with the soy sauce. Bring the mixture to the boil and
 simmer for 4–5 minutes until the liquid has reduced
 and thickened.

4 Add the tomatoes and coriander and cook for 1–2
 minutes before serving with noodles or rice.

variation

Instead of the fresh coriander, use kaffir lime leaves, finely
slivered, and the zest and juice of a lime to add a unique
aroma to the dish.

asian pork

ingredients

serves 4

450 g/1 lb lean boneless pork
1½ tbsp plain flour
1–2 tbsp olive oil
1 onion, cut into small wedges
2–3 garlic cloves, chopped
2.5-cm/1-inch piece fresh
    ginger, peeled and grated
1 tbsp tomato purée
300 ml/10 fl oz chicken stock
225 g/8 oz canned pineapple
    chunks in natural juice
1–1½ tbsp dark soy sauce
1 red pepper, deseeded and sliced
1 green pepper, deseeded and
    sliced
1½ tbsp balsamic vinegar
4 spring onions, diagonally sliced,
    to garnish

method

1 Trim off any fat or gristle from the pork and cut into
2.5-cm/1-inch chunks. Toss the pork in the flour until
well coated and reserve any remaining flour.

2 Heat the oil in a large, heavy-based saucepan and
cook the onion, garlic and ginger, stirring frequently,
for 5 minutes, or until softened. Add the pork and
cook over a high heat, stirring frequently, for 5 minutes,
or until browned on all sides and sealed. Sprinkle in
the reserved flour and cook, stirring constantly, for
2 minutes, then remove from the heat.

3 Blend the tomato purée with the stock in a heatproof
jug and gradually stir into the saucepan. Drain the
pineapple, reserving both the fruit and juice, and stir
the juice into the saucepan.

4 Add the soy sauce to the saucepan, then return to the
heat and bring to the boil, stirring. Reduce the heat,
cover and simmer, stirring occasionally, for 1 hour.
Add the peppers and cook for a further 15 minutes,
or until the pork is tender. Stir in the vinegar and the
pineapple and heat through for 5 minutes. Serve
sprinkled with the spring onions.

paprika pork

ingredients

serves 4

675 g/1 lb 8 oz pork fillet
2 tbsp sunflower oil
25 g/1 oz butter
1 onion, chopped
1 tbsp paprika
25 g/1 oz plain flour
300 ml/10 fl oz chicken stock
4 tbsp dry sherry
115 g/4 oz mushrooms, sliced
150 ml/5 fl oz soured cream
salt and pepper

method

1 Cut the pork into 4-cm/1½-inch cubes. Heat the oil and butter in a large saucepan. Add the pork and cook over a medium heat, stirring, for 5 minutes, or until browned. Transfer to a plate with a slotted spoon.

2 Add the chopped onion to the saucepan and cook, stirring occasionally, for 5 minutes, or until softened. Stir in the paprika and flour and cook, stirring constantly, for 2 minutes. Gradually stir in the stock and bring to the boil, stirring constantly.

3 Return the pork to the saucepan, add the sherry and sliced mushrooms and season to taste with salt and pepper. Cover and simmer gently for 20 minutes, or until the pork is tender. Stir in the soured cream and serve.

red roasted pork with peppered noodles

ingredients

serves 2

1 tbsp Thai red curry paste
2 tbsp soy sauce
350 g/12 oz pork fillet, trimmed
225 g/8 oz fine dried egg noodles
2 tbsp groundnut or vegetable oil
1 red onion, chopped
2.5-cm/1-inch piece fresh ginger,
   finely chopped
1 garlic clove, finely chopped
1 orange pepper, deseeded
   and chopped
1 red pepper, deseeded
   and chopped
1 tsp pepper
1 small bunch of fresh chives,
   snipped
handful of fresh coriander,
   chopped

method

1 Mix the curry paste and soy sauce together in a small bowl and spread over the pork fillet. Cover and leave to marinate in the refrigerator for 1 hour.

2 Preheat the oven to 200°C/400°F/Gas Mark 6. Roast the pork in the preheated oven for 20–25 minutes, until cooked through. Remove from the oven, cover with foil and leave to rest for 15 minutes.

3 Meanwhile, cook the noodles in a large saucepan of boiling water for 4 minutes, or according to the packet instructions, until just tender. Drain, rinse under cold running water and set aside.

4 Heat the oil in a preheated wok, add the onion, ginger and garlic and stir-fry over a medium–high heat for 1–2 minutes. Add the orange and red peppers and pepper and stir-fry for 2–3 minutes, until tender. Stir in the chives and most of the coriander.

5 Add the drained noodles to the pepper mixture and toss together until well mixed. Divide between 2 serving dishes. Slice the pork and arrange on top of the noodles. Scatter with the remaining coriander and serve immediately.

pork & pasta bake

ingredients

serves 4

2 tbsp olive oil

1 onion, chopped

1 garlic clove, finely chopped

2 carrots, diced

55 g/2 oz pancetta, chopped

115 g/4 oz mushrooms, chopped

450 g/1 lb fresh pork mince

125 ml/4 fl oz dry white wine

4 tbsp passata

200 g/7 oz canned chopped tomatoes

2 tsp chopped fresh sage, plus extra sprigs to garnish

225 g/8 oz dried penne

140 g/5 oz mozzarella cheese, diced

4 tbsp freshly grated Parmesan

300 ml/10 fl oz ready-made Béchamel sauce

salt and pepper

method

1 Preheat the oven to 200°C/400°F/Gas Mark 6. Heat the oil in a large heavy-based frying pan. Add the onion, garlic and carrots and cook over a low heat, stirring occasionally, for 5 minutes, or until the onion has softened. Add the pancetta and cook for 5 minutes. Add the chopped mushrooms and cook for a further 2 minutes. Add the pork and cook, breaking it up with a wooden spoon, until the meat is browned all over. Stir in the wine, passata, chopped tomatoes and their can juices and chopped sage. Season to taste with salt and pepper, bring to the boil, then cover and simmer over a low heat for 25–30 minutes.

2 Meanwhile, bring a large heavy-based saucepan of lightly salted water to the boil. Add the pasta, return to the boil and cook for 8–10 minutes, or until tender but still firm to the bite.

3 Spoon the pork mixture into a large ovenproof dish. Stir the mozzarella cheese and half the Parmesan cheese into the Béchamel sauce. Drain the pasta and stir the sauce into it, then spoon it over the pork mixture. Sprinkle with the remaining Parmesan cheese and bake in the preheated oven for 25–30 minutes, or until golden brown. Serve immediately, garnished with sage sprigs.

quiche lorraine

ingredients

serves 6

pastry

175 g/6 oz plain flour, plus
   extra for dusting
pinch of salt
115 g/4 oz butter, diced
25 g/1 oz pecorino cheese, grated
4–6 tbsp iced water

filling

115 g/4 oz Gruyère cheese,
   thinly sliced
55 g/2 oz Roquefort cheese,
   crumbled
175 g/6 oz rindless lean bacon,
   grilled until crisp
3 eggs
150 ml/5 fl oz double cream
salt and pepper

method

1 To make the pastry, sift the flour with the salt into a
   bowl. Add the butter and rub it in with your fingertips
   until the mixture resembles fine breadcrumbs. Stir in
   the grated cheese, then stir in enough of the water to
   bind. Shape the dough into a ball, wrap in foil and chill
   in the refrigerator for 15 minutes.

2 Preheat the oven to 190°C/375°F/Gas Mark 5. Unwrap
   and roll out the dough on a lightly floured work surface.
   Use to line a 23-cm/9-inch quiche tin. Place the tin on
   a baking sheet. Prick the base of the pastry case all over
   with a fork, line with foil or greaseproof paper and fill
   with baking beans. Bake in the preheated oven for
   15 minutes until the edges are set and dry. Remove the
   beans and lining and bake the pastry case for a further
   5–7 minutes, or until golden. Leave to cool slightly.

3 For the filling, arrange the cheeses over the base of the
   pastry case, then crumble the bacon evenly on top.
   Place the eggs and cream in a bowl and beat together
   until combined. Add salt and pepper to taste. Pour the
   mixture into the pastry case and return to the oven for
   20 minutes, or until the filling is golden and set.

4 Remove from the oven and cool the quiche in the tin
   for 10 minutes. Transfer to a wire rack to cool and serve
   at room temperature.

pea, ham & crème fraîche tartlets

ingredients

serves 6

pastry

70 g/2½ oz butter, diced and
　　chilled, plus extra for greasing
125 g/4½ oz plain flour,
　　plus extra for dusting
pinch of salt
25 g/1 oz freshly grated
　　Parmesan cheese
1–2 tbsp iced water

filling

200 g/7 oz fresh or frozen peas
25 g/1 oz unsalted butter
2 shallots, finely chopped
100 g/3½ oz cooked ham,
　　chopped
3–4 fresh mint leaves, chopped
125 ml/4 fl oz crème fraîche
3 egg yolks
salt and pepper

method

1 Grease 6 x 9-cm/3½-inch loose-based fluted tart tins.
To make the pastry, sift the flour and salt into a bowl
and rub in the butter with your fingertips until the
mixture resembles fine breadcrumbs. Stir in the
Parmesan cheese and mix in a little iced water, just
enough to bring the dough together.

2 Turn out onto a lightly floured work surface and cut
into 6 equal-sized pieces. Roll out each piece and use
to line each tart tin, pressing to fit. Roll the rolling pin
over the tins to neaten the edges and trim the excess
pastry. Put a piece of baking paper into each tartlet and
fill with baking beans. Chill for 30 minutes. Meanwhile,
preheat the oven to 200°C/400°F/Gas Mark 6. Bake the
tartlet cases in the preheated oven for 10 minutes, then
remove the paper and beans.

3 To make the filling, cook the peas in boiling water for
3–4 minutes, then drain. Melt the butter in a frying pan,
add the shallots and cook for 10 minutes. Add the ham
and cook for 3–5 minutes. Add the peas and mint,
remove from the heat and stir in the crème fraîche and
egg yolks. Season to taste. Divide between the tartlet
cases. Bake for 12–15 minutes. Transfer to a wire rack
to cool and serve at room temperature.

artichoke & pancetta tartlets

ingredients

serves 6

70 g/2½ oz butter, diced and
    chilled, plus extra for greasing
125 g/4½ oz plain flour, plus extra
    for dusting
pinch of salt
1–2 tbsp iced water

filling

5 tbsp double cream
4 tbsp bottled artichoke paste,
    tapenade or pesto
400 g/14 oz canned artichoke
    hearts, drained
12 thin-cut pancetta rashers
salt and pepper

to serve

rocket leaves
50 g/1¾ oz Parmesan
    or pecorino cheese
2 tbsp olive oil, for drizzling

method

1 Grease 6 x 9-cm/3½-inch loose-based fluted tart tins.
To make the pastry, sift the flour and salt into a bowl
and rub in the butter with your fingertips until the
mixture resembles fine breadcrumbs. Mix in a little
iced water, just enough to bring the dough together.

2 Turn out onto a lightly floured work surface and cut
into 6 equal-sized pieces. Roll out each piece and use
to line each tart tin, pressing to fit. Roll the rolling pin
over the tins to neaten the edges and trim the excess
pastry. Put a piece of baking paper into each tartlet
and fill with baking beans. Chill for 30 minutes.
Meanwhile, preheat the oven to 200°C/400°F/Gas
Mark 6. Bake the tartlet cases in the preheated oven
for 10 minutes, then remove the paper and beans.

3 To make the filling, stir the cream and artichoke paste
together in a bowl and season well with salt and
pepper. Divide between the tartlet cases, spreading
out to cover the base of each tartlet. Cut each
artichoke heart into 3 pieces and divide between the
tartlets. Curl 2 rashers of the pancetta into each tart.
Bake for 10 minutes.

4 To serve, top each tartlet with a few rocket leaves.
Shave the Parmesan cheese and scatter the shavings
over the tartlets. Drizzle with oil and serve.

sausage & bean casserole

ingredients

serves 4

8 Italian sausages
3 tbsp olive oil
1 large onion, chopped
2 garlic cloves, chopped
1 green pepper, deseeded
    and sliced
400 g/14 oz canned chopped
    tomatoes
2 tbsp sun-dried tomato purée
400 g/14 oz canned cannellini
    beans, drained and rinsed

method

1 Prick the sausages all over with a fork. Heat 2 tablespoons of the oil in a large, heavy-based frying pan. Add the sausages and cook over a low heat, turning frequently, for 10–15 minutes, until evenly browned and cooked through. Remove them from the frying pan and keep warm. Drain off the oil and wipe out the pan with kitchen paper.

2 Heat the remaining oil in the frying pan. Add the onion, garlic and pepper to the frying pan and cook for 5 minutes, stirring occasionally, or until softened.

3 Add the tomatoes to the frying pan and leave the mixture to simmer for about 5 minutes, stirring occasionally, or until slightly reduced and thickened.

4 Stir the sun-dried tomato purée, cannellini beans and Italian sausages into the mixture in the frying pan. Cook for 4–5 minutes or until the mixture is piping hot. Add 4–5 tablespoons of water if the mixture becomes too dry during cooking. Transfer to serving plates and serve.

puy lentils with sausages

ingredients

serves 4–6

2 tbsp sunflower oil,
    plus extra for brushing
1 large onion, finely chopped
2 large garlic cloves,
    finely chopped
2 carrots, cut into 5-mm/
    ¼-inch dice
400 g/14 oz Puy lentils, rinsed
½ tsp dried thyme
1 bay leaf
8–12 fresh sausages, such
    as Toulouse
50 ml/2 fl oz vinaigrette
2 tbsp chopped fresh
    flat-leaf parsley
salt and pepper

method

1 Heat the oil in a heavy-based saucepan with a tight-fitting lid over a medium–high heat. Add the chopped onion, garlic and carrots and cook, stirring frequently, for 5 minutes, or until the onion is softened but not browned.

2 Stir in the lentils. Add enough water to cover the lentils by 2.5 cm/1 inch and bring to the boil, skimming the surface with a spoon, if necessary. Stir in the thyme and bay leaf, then reduce the heat to low, cover and leave to simmer for 10 minutes. Uncover the saucepan and simmer for a further 15–20 minutes, or until the carrots and lentils are tender.

3 Meanwhile, preheat the grill to high. Brush the grill rack with oil. Lightly prick the sausages all over and cook under the preheated grill, turning occasionally, until cooked through and the skins are crisp and brown. Set aside and keep warm.

4 The lentils should absorb all the water by the time they are tender, but if any remains on the surface, drain it off. Transfer the lentils to a large serving bowl. Add the vinaigrette to the hot lentils and stir so that they are well coated.

5 Add salt and pepper to taste, then stir in the parsley. Serve the hot lentils with the sausages.

pork hotpot

ingredients

serves 6

85 g/3 oz plain flour
1.3 kg/3 lb pork fillet, cut
    into 5-mm/¼-inch slices
4 tbsp sunflower oil
2 onions, thinly sliced
2 garlic cloves, finely chopped
400 g/14 oz canned chopped
    tomatoes in juice
350 ml/12 fl oz dry white wine
1 tbsp torn fresh basil leaves
2 tbsp chopped fresh parsley,
    plus extra sprigs to garnish
salt and pepper
fresh crusty bread, to serve

method

1 Spread the flour out on a plate and season to taste with salt and pepper. Toss the pork slices in the flour to coat, shaking off any excess. Heat the oil in a flameproof casserole over a medium heat. Add the pork slices and cook until browned all over. Using a slotted spoon, transfer the pork to a plate.

2 Add the onions to the casserole and cook over a low heat, stirring occasionally, for 10 minutes, or until golden brown. Add the garlic and cook, stirring, for 2 minutes, then add the tomatoes with their juice, the wine and basil leaves and season to taste with salt and pepper. Cook, stirring frequently, for 3 minutes.

3 Return the pork to the casserole, cover and simmer gently for 1 hour, or until the meat is tender. Stir in the chopped parsley.

4 Serve immediately, garnished with parsley sprigs and accompanied by fresh crusty bread.

marinated pork with garlic

ingredients

serves 6

5 tbsp rice vinegar

4 tbsp dark soy sauce

1 tbsp coriander seeds, crushed

1 kg/2 lb 4 oz boneless pork, cut into 2.5–4-cm/ 1–1½-inch cubes

1 garlic bulb, separated into cloves and peeled

2 tbsp groundnut or sunflower oil

350 g/12 oz sweet potatoes, peeled and cubed

8 black peppercorns, lightly crushed

stir-fried cabbage, to serve

method

1 Mix the vinegar, soy sauce and crushed coriander seeds together in a shallow, non-metallic dish. Add the pork cubes and turn to coat in the marinade. Cover and leave to marinate in the refrigerator for 1 hour.

2 Slice the garlic cloves lengthways. Remove the pork from the marinade, reserving the marinade. Heat the oil in a heavy-based saucepan over a high heat. Add the garlic and cook, stirring, for 1 minute. Reduce the heat to medium, add the pork and cook, stirring, for 5 minutes. Add the sweet potatoes, peppercorns, the reserved marinade and water to cover. Bring to the boil, skim off any foam that rises to the surface, then reduce the heat, cover and simmer for 30 minutes.

3 Uncover the pan, increase the heat to high and cook, stirring frequently, for 25 minutes, or until the pork is tender and the sauce is slightly thickened. Serve hot with stir-fried cabbage.

game

chicken & pasta soup with guinea fowl

ingredients

serves 2–4

500 g/1 lb 2 oz skinless, boneless chicken, chopped

500 g/1 lb 2 oz skinless, boneless guinea fowl, chopped

600 ml/1 pint chicken stock

1 small onion, quartered

6 peppercorns

1 tsp cloves

pinch of mace

150 ml/5 fl oz double cream

15 g/¹/₂ oz butter

2 tsp plain flour

125 g/4¹/₂ oz dried spaghetti, broken into short lengths and cooked

2 tbsp chopped fresh parsley, to garnish

method

1 Put the chicken and guinea fowl in a large saucepan with the stock. Bring to the boil and add the onion, peppercorns, cloves and mace. Reduce the heat and simmer gently for 2 hours, or until the stock is reduced by one third.

2 Sieve the soup and skim off any fat. Return the soup and meat to a clean saucepan. Add the cream and slowly bring to the boil.

3 To make a roux, melt the butter in a small saucepan over a low heat. Add the flour and cook, stirring constantly, until it forms a paste-like consistency. Add the roux to the soup and cook, stirring constantly, until slightly thickened.

4 Just before serving, stir in the cooked spaghetti.

5 Ladle the soup into individual warmed serving bowls, garnish with the chopped parsley and serve.

guinea fowl with cabbage

ingredients

serves 4

1 oven-ready guinea fowl,
    weighing 1.25 kg/2 lb 12 oz
½ tbsp sunflower oil
½ apple, peeled, cored
    and chopped
several fresh flat-leaf parsley
    sprigs, stems bruised
1 large Savoy cabbage, coarse
    outer leaves discarded,
    cored and quartered
1 thick piece smoked belly of
    pork, about 140 g/5 oz, rind
    removed, cut into thin lardons,
    or 140 g/5 oz unsmoked
    lardons
1 onion, sliced
1 bouquet garni sachet
1½ tbsp chopped fresh
    flat-leaf parsley
salt and pepper

method

1 Preheat the oven to 240°C/475°F/Gas Mark 9. Rub the
guinea fowl with the oil and season to taste inside and
out with salt and pepper. Put the apple and parsley
sprigs in the cavity and truss to tie the legs together.
Put in a roasting tin and roast in the preheated oven
for 20 minutes, or until the breast is golden brown.
Immediately reduce the temperature to 160°C/325°F/
Gas Mark 3.

2 Meanwhile, blanch the cabbage in boiling water for
3 minutes. Drain, rinse in cold water and pat dry.

3 Put the lardons in a flameproof casserole over a
medium–high heat and cook until the fat runs.
Remove with a slotted spoon and set aside. Add the
onion and cook, stirring frequently, for 5 minutes, or
until softened but not browned. Add the bouquet
garni with a very little salt and a pinch of pepper, then
return the lardons to the casserole with the cabbage.
Top with the guinea fowl. Cover with a piece of wet
greaseproof paper, then add the lid and cook in the
preheated oven for 45–60 minutes, or until the guinea
fowl is tender and the juices run clear when a skewer
is inserted into the thickest part of the meat.

4 Cut the guinea fowl into portions. Stir the parsley into
the cabbage and onion and serve with the meat.

roast pheasant with red wine & herbs

ingredients

serves 4

100 g/3½ oz butter,
    slightly softened
1 tbsp chopped fresh thyme
1 tbsp chopped fresh parsley
2 oven-ready young pheasants
4 tbsp vegetable oil
125 ml/4 fl oz red wine
salt and pepper
roast parsnips and potatoes,
    to serve

method

1 Preheat the oven to 190°C/375°F/Gas Mark 5. Place the butter in a small bowl and mix in the chopped herbs. Lift the skins off the pheasants, taking care not to tear them, and push the herb butter under the skins. Season to taste with salt and pepper.

2 Pour the oil into a roasting tin, add the pheasants and cook in the preheated oven for 45 minutes, basting occasionally. Remove from the oven, pour over the red wine, then return to the oven and cook for a further 15 minutes, or until cooked through. Check that each bird is cooked by inserting a knife between the legs and body. If the juices run clear, they are cooked.

3 Remove the pheasants from the oven, cover with foil and leave to stand for 15 minutes. Divide among individual serving plates, and serve with roast parsnips and potatoes.

pesto-baked partridge

ingredients

serves 4

8 partridge pieces, about
115 g/4 oz each
55 g/2 oz butter, melted
4 tbsp Dijon mustard
2 tbsp lime juice
1 tbsp brown sugar
6 tbsp green pesto sauce
450 g/1 lb dried rigatoni
1 tbsp olive oil
115 g/4 oz freshly grated
Parmesan cheese
salt and pepper

method

1 Preheat the oven to 200°C/400°F/Gas Mark 6. Arrange the partridge pieces, smooth side down, in a single layer in a large, ovenproof dish.

2 Mix together the butter, mustard, lime juice and sugar in a bowl. Season to taste with salt and pepper. Brush some of this mixture over the partridge pieces and bake in the preheated oven for 15 minutes.

3 Remove the dish from the oven and coat the partridge pieces with 3 tablespoons of the green pesto sauce. Return to the oven and bake for a further 12 minutes.

4 Remove the dish from the oven and carefully turn over the partridge pieces. Coat the top of the partridge pieces with the remaining mustard mixture and return to the oven for a further 10 minutes.

5 Meanwhile, bring a large, heavy-based saucepan of lightly salted water to the boil. Add the rigatoni and oil and cook for 8–10 minutes, until the pasta is tender but still firm to the bite. Drain and transfer to a warmed serving dish and toss with the remaining green pesto sauce and the grated Parmesan cheese.

6 Serve the partridge with the pasta, pouring over the cooking juices.

goose with honey & pears

ingredients

serves 4

1 oven-ready goose, weighing
    3.5–4.5 kg /7 lb 12 oz–10 lb
1 tsp salt
4 pears
1 tbsp lemon juice
55 g/2 oz butter
2 tbsp honey
lemon slices, to garnish
seasonal vegetables, to serve

method

1 Preheat the oven to 220°C/425°F/Gas Mark 7.

2 Rinse the goose and pat dry. Use a fork to prick the skin all over, then rub with the salt. Place the bird upside down on a rack in a roasting pan. Roast in the oven for 30 minutes. Drain off the fat. Turn the bird over and roast for 15 minutes. Drain off the fat again. Reduce the temperature to 180°C/350°F/Gas Mark 4 and roast for 15 minutes per 450 g/1 lb. Cover with foil 15 minutes before the end of the cooking time. Check that the bird is cooked by inserting a knife between the legs and body. If the juices run clear, it is cooked. Remove from the oven and keep warm.

3 Peel and halve the pears and brush with lemon juice. Melt the butter and honey in a pan over low heat, then add the pears. Cook, stirring, for 5–10 minutes until tender. Remove from the heat, arrange the pears around the goose, and pour the sweet juices over the bird. Garnish the dish with lemon slices and serve with seasonal vegetables.

roast goose with cinnamon-spiced red cabbage

ingredients

serves 6

1 oven-ready goose, weighing about 4.5 kg/10 lb
2 onions, quartered
2 bay leaves
1 bunch fresh thyme
salt and pepper

red cabbage

3 tbsp olive oil
1 large onion, sliced
1 red cabbage, shredded
1 large cooking apple, peeled, cored and chopped
3 tbsp raisins
300 ml/10 fl oz red wine
50 ml/2 fl oz red wine vinegar
2 tsp caster sugar, or to taste
1 cinnamon stick

method

1 Preheat the oven to 200°C/400°F/Gas Mark 6.

2 Cut away any excess fat from the tail area of the goose. Season the goose cavity to taste with salt and pepper and push in the onion quarters, bay leaves and thyme, reserving a few sprigs for the garnish. Put the goose on a rack set over a roasting tin and prick the skin all over with a skewer. Season the outside of the goose to taste with salt and pepper. Roast in the preheated oven for 15 minutes per 450 g/1 lb, plus an extra 15 minutes. Remove from the oven, cover loosely with foil and leave to rest for 15 minutes before carving.

3 While the goose is roasting, prepare the red cabbage. Heat the oil in a large frying pan over a medium heat, add the onion and cook, stirring frequently, for 3–4 minutes until softened but not coloured. Add all the remaining ingredients, cover and cook for 30–40 minutes until the cabbage is tender and the liquid has reduced. Remove the cinnamon stick before serving.

4 Carve the goose and serve in slices, alongside the red cabbage and garnished with the reserved thyme.

quails with grapes

ingredients

serves 4

600 g/1 lb 5 oz potatoes,
    peeled
4 tbsp olive oil, plus extra
    for frying
8 quails, gutted
280 g/10 oz green seedless grapes
225 ml/8 fl oz grape juice
2 cloves
about 150 ml/5 fl oz water
2 tbsp Spanish brandy
salt and pepper

method

1 Preheat the oven to 230°C/450°F/Gas Mark 8. Par-boil
   the potatoes for 10 minutes. Drain and leave to cool
   completely. Reserve until required.

2 Take a flameproof casserole large enough to hold the
   quails in a single layer and heat the oil over a medium
   heat. Add the quails and fry on all sides until they are
   golden brown. Spoon off some of the oil for frying
   the potatoes.

3 Add the grapes, grape juice, cloves, enough water to
   come halfway up the side of the quails, and salt and
   pepper to taste. Cover and simmer for 20 minutes.
   Transfer the quails and all the juices to a casserole,
   and sprinkle the brandy over the quails. Roast,
   uncovered, in the preheated oven for 10 minutes.

4 Pan-fry the par-boiled potatoes in the quail oil, adding
   extra olive oil if needed. Place the potatoes on
   individual serving plates.

5 Place 2 quails on top of the pan-fried potatoes on each
   of the individual serving plates. Taste the grape sauce
   and adjust the seasoning if necessary. Spoon the sauce
   over the quails and serve immediately with crispy
   pan-fried potatoes.

game pie

ingredients

serves 4–6

oil, for greasing
700 g/1 lb 9 oz mixed game,
    cut into 3-cm/1¼-inch pieces
2 tbsp plain flour, plus extra
    for dusting
3 tbsp vegetable oil
1 onion, roughly chopped
1 garlic clove, finely chopped
350 g/12 oz large field
    mushrooms, sliced
1 tsp crushed juniper berries
125 ml/4 fl oz port or Marsala
450 ml/16 fl oz chicken
    or game stock
400 g/14 oz ready-made
    puff pastry
1 egg, beaten
salt and pepper

method

1 Preheat the oven to 160°C/325°F/Gas Mark 3. Grease a 1.2-litre/2-pint pie dish. Put the meat into a large plastic bag with the flour and salt and pepper and shake to coat the meat.

2 Heat the oil in a large flameproof casserole dish over a high heat and brown the meat in batches. Fry the onion and garlic until softened, then add the mushrooms and cook, stirring constantly. Add the juniper berries, port and stock, stirring constantly, and bring to the boil for 2–3 minutes. Return the meat to the casserole. Cover and cook in the oven for 1½–2 hours until the meat is tender. Remove from the oven and cool. Chill overnight in the refrigerator to develop the flavours.

3 Preheat the oven to 200°C/400°F/Gas Mark 6. Roll out the pastry on a lightly floured work surface to about 7 cm/2¾ inches larger than the pie dish. Cut off a 3-cm/1¼-inch strip around the edge. Moisten the rim of the dish and press the pastry strip onto it. Place a pie funnel in the centre of the dish and spoon in the meat filling. Moisten the pastry strip with a little water and put on the pastry lid. Crimp the edges of the pastry firmly and glaze with the egg.

4 Bake the pie on a tray near the top of the oven for 30 minutes. Serve golden brown and bubbling hot.

chargrilled venison steaks

ingredients

serves 4

4 venison steaks
150 ml/5 fl oz red wine
2 tbsp sunflower oil
1 tbsp red wine vinegar
1 onion, chopped
fresh parsley sprigs
2 fresh thyme sprigs, plus
    extra sprigs to garnish
1 bay leaf
1 tsp caster sugar
$\frac{1}{2}$ tsp mild mustard
salt and pepper
baked potatoes, to serve

method

1 Place the venison steaks in a shallow, non-metallic dish.

2 Combine the wine, oil, wine vinegar, onion, fresh parsley, thyme, bay leaf, sugar and mustard, and salt and pepper to taste, in a screw-top jar. Shake vigorously until well combined. Alternatively, using a fork, whisk the ingredients together in a bowl.

3 Pour the marinade mixture over the venison, cover and leave to marinate in the refrigerator overnight. Turn the steaks over in the mixture occasionally so that the meat is well coated.

4 Preheat the barbecue or grill to high. Cook the venison over hot coals, sealing the meat over the hottest part of the barbecue for 2 minutes on each side. Alternatively, cook under the hot grill for the same amount of time.

5 Move the meat to an area with slightly less intense heat, or turn down the grill to medium, and cook for a further 4–10 minutes on each side, according to taste. Test the meat by inserting the tip of a knife into the meat – the juices will range from red when the meat is still rare to clear as the meat becomes well cooked.

6 Transfer the venison steaks to serving plates, garnish with fresh thyme sprigs and serve with baked potatoes.

roast venison with brandy sauce

ingredients

serves 4

6 tbsp vegetable oil
1 saddle of fresh venison,
    weighing 1.7 kg/3 lb 12 oz,
    trimmed
salt and pepper
fresh thyme sprigs, to garnish
selection of vegetables,
    to serve

brandy sauce
1 tbsp plain flour
4 tbsp vegetable stock
175 ml/6 fl oz brandy
100 ml/3½ fl oz double cream

method

1 Preheat the oven to 180°C/350°F/Gas Mark 4.

2 Heat half the oil in a frying pan over a high heat.
   Season the venison to taste with salt and pepper, add
   to the pan and cook until lightly browned all over. Pour
   the remaining oil into a roasting tin. Add the venison,
   cover with foil and roast in the preheated oven, basting
   occasionally, for 1½ hours, or until cooked through.
   Remove from the oven and transfer to a warmed
   serving platter. Cover loosely with foil and leave to rest.

3 To make the sauce, stir the flour into the roasting tin
   over a medium heat and cook, stirring constantly, for
   1 minute. Stir in the stock, scraping the sediment from
   the base of the tin. Gradually stir in the brandy and
   bring to the boil, then reduce the heat and simmer,
   stirring frequently, for 10 minutes, or until the sauce
   has thickened a little. Remove from the heat and stir
   in the cream.

4 Garnish the venison with thyme sprigs and serve with
   the brandy sauce and a selection of vegetables.

venison casserole

ingredients

serves 4–6

3 tbsp olive oil
1 kg/2 lb 4 oz casserole venison,
    cut into 3-cm/1¼-inch cubes
2 onions, thinly sliced
2 garlic cloves, chopped
2 tbsp plain flour
350 ml/12 fl oz beef or
    vegetable stock
125 ml/4 fl oz port or red wine
2 tbsp redcurrant jelly
6 juniper berries, crushed
pinch of ground cinnamon
freshly grated nutmeg
175 g/6 oz vacuum-packed
    chestnuts (optional)
salt and pepper
baked potatoes, to serve

method

1 Preheat the oven to 150°C/300°F/Gas Mark 2.

2 Heat the oil in a large frying pan over a high heat.
Add the venison, in batches if necessary, and cook
until browned all over. Using a slotted spoon, transfer
to a large casserole.

3 Add the onions and garlic to the frying pan and cook
over a medium heat, stirring frequently, for 8 minutes,
or until golden. Transfer to the casserole. Sprinkle the
venison in the casserole with the flour and turn to
coat evenly.

4 Gradually add the stock to the frying pan, stirring well
and scraping the sediment from the base of the frying
pan, then bring to the boil. Transfer to the casserole
and stir well, ensuring that the meat is just covered.

5 Add the port, redcurrant jelly, juniper berries,
cinnamon, a little freshly grated nutmeg and the
chestnuts, if using. Season well with salt and pepper
and stir well. Cover and cook in the centre of the
preheated oven for 2–2½ hours.

6 Remove from the oven and adjust the seasoning,
if necessary. Serve immediately, piping hot, with
baked potatoes.

rabbit with prunes

ingredients

serves 4-6

2 tablespoons plain flour

1 rabbit, weighing 1.25 kg/
2 lb 12 oz, cut into 8 pieces

25 g/1 oz unsalted butter

1 tbsp sunflower oil

2 shallots, finely chopped

1 large tomato, peeled, deseeded
and diced

1 large garlic clove, crushed

250 ml/9 fl oz full-bodied
red wine

250 ml/9 fl oz water

3 cloves

3 black peppercorns, crushed

½ tsp ground ginger

¼ tsp ground cinnamon

12–16 ready-to-eat prunes

3 tbsp raisins

salt and pepper

chopped fresh flat-leaf parsley,
to garnish

method

1 Put the flour with salt and pepper to taste in a polythene bag, add the rabbit pieces and shake well to coat each piece.

2 Melt the butter with the oil in a large sauté or frying pan with a tight-fitting lid or a flameproof casserole over a medium–high heat. Add the rabbit pieces and cook until lightly browned all over. Transfer to a plate. Add the shallots, tomato and garlic to the pan and cook, stirring frequently, for 3 minutes, or until the shallots are softened. Return the rabbit pieces to the pan. Add the wine and water to just cover the rabbit.

3 Stir in the cloves, peppercorns, ginger, cinnamon and salt and pepper to taste. Bring to the boil, stirring, then reduce the heat to low, cover and simmer for 45 minutes. Stir in the prunes and raisins, cover and simmer for a further 15 minutes, or until the rabbit pieces are tender when pierced with the tip of a knife.

4 Transfer the rabbit pieces to a serving platter, cover loosely with foil and keep warm. Bring the sauce to the boil and leave to bubble and reduce for 2–3 minutes until it has a coating consistency. Taste and adjust the seasoning, if necessary.

5 Serve the rabbit pieces with the sauce and fruit spooned over, garnished with chopped parsley.

rabbit, roast tomato & sage pie

ingredients

serves 4

450 g/1 lb cherry tomatoes
3 tbsp olive oil
½ tsp sugar
1 tbsp plain flour
700 g/1 lb 9 oz boned rabbit,
  cubed
1 onion, chopped
1 garlic clove, finely chopped
25 g/1 oz pine kernels
150 ml/5 fl oz chicken or
  vegetable stock
1 tbsp lemon juice
12 fresh sage leaves, finely
  chopped
35 g/1¼ oz butter
100 g/3½ oz ready-made filo
  pastry
salt and pepper

method

1 Preheat the oven to 200°C/400°F/Gas Mark 6. Put the tomatoes in a roasting tin and sprinkle with 1 tablespoon of the oil and the sugar. Roast for 30 minutes.

2 Meanwhile, put the flour in a polythene bag, add the rabbit and shake well to coat each piece. Heat 1 tablespoon of the remaining oil in a large, heavy-based frying pan over a medium heat. Add the onion and garlic and cook until softened. Add the pine kernels and cook, stirring frequently. Using a slotted spoon, transfer the mixture to a 1.4-litre/2½-pint pie dish.

3 Heat the remaining oil in the frying pan over a medium–high heat. Add the rabbit and cook until browned all over. Add the stock and lemon juice and bring to the boil, stirring constantly. Reduce the heat and simmer for 2–3 minutes. Transfer to the pie dish.

4 When the tomatoes have roasted, gently stir them into the pie dish. Add the sage and season to taste with salt and pepper. Reduce the oven temperature to 190°C/375°F/Gas Mark 5. Melt the butter in a saucepan over a low heat. Take one sheet of pastry and brush the sheet with a little of the melted butter, then cut into 2.5-cm/1-inch strips. Arrange on top of the pie. Repeat with the remaining pastry sheets. Bake the pie in the oven for 30 minutes, or until golden brown. Serve hot.

index